Robert Crawford

South American Sketches

Robert Crawford

South American Sketches

ISBN/EAN: 9783743331631

Manufactured in Europe, USA, Canada, Australia, Japa

Cover: Foto ©Andreas Hilbeck / pixelio.de

Manufactured and distributed by brebook publishing software (www.brebook.com)

Robert Crawford

South American Sketches

SOUTH AMERICAN SKETCHES

BY

ROBERT CRAWFORD, M.A.

HONORARY MASTER IN ENGINEERING, DUBLIN UNIVERSITY
MEMBER OF THE INSTITUTION OF CIVIL ENGINEERS
MEMBER OF THE ROYAL IRISH ACADEMY
ETC. ETC.

Author of "*Across the Pampas and the Andes*"
"*Reminiscences of Foreign Travel,*" *etc.*

LONGMANS, GREEN, AND CO.
39 PATERNOSTER ROW, LONDON
NEW YORK AND BOMBAY
1898

All rights reserved

PREFACE

ALTHOUGH this volume had its origin in a visit to South America, resulting in a residence in Uruguay for three and a half years, ending in 1892, the incidents related in it, and the information it conveys, are not confined to that period. Of those narratives that do not recount the writer's personal experience some occurred before the time in question, others since then.

As regards the railways of Uruguay, the information concerning them is brought down to the present date; and the same may be said of the part of the contents which relates to the general condition of that country.

Uruguay has suffered much of late from a revolution, which seriously retarded its progress; but as peace has been concluded, it is to be hoped that good government and wise reforms may ensue, and the country be left undisturbed in the future to attain to the prosperity for which it is so eminently suited by position, soil, and climate.

Although the headquarters of the reader's thoughts during the perusal of this volume will be in Uruguay, his attention will not be exclusively confined within the limits of that republic. Many of the narratives contained in the following pages refer to occurrences in other places. This explanation seems necessary in consequence of the strong family likeness existing in the incidents of public and political life all throughout South America, which might easily cause the history of current events in one part of that continent to be mistaken for that belonging to another.

ROBERT CRAWFORD.

STONEWOLD, BALLYSHANNON,
March 1898.

CONTENTS

CHAPTER I

INTRODUCTION

PAGE

It is always the unexpected that happens—Wisdom in epigrammatic form—We don't possess the gift of prophecy—Unanticipated events occur with sufficient frequency—My own experience—A railway in Uruguay—A country with opposite characteristics—Altering the position of the moral—Advantages of civility—A civil letter-writer—Results—Indirect certificate of character for urbanity—*Suaviter in modo* not always successful—*Fortiter in re* sometimes necessary 1–8

CHAPTER II

"A LIFE ON THE OCEAN WAVE"

The voyage begins—Carril and Vigo—Embarking emigrants—Spanish officials—Lisbon—More emigrants—Off to St. Vincent—Across the Atlantic—Fellow-passengers—A caterer for the general amusement—The centre of attraction—Disadvantages of the best position—Professor M——'s "Principles of the Art of Conversation"—Wasted moments—Unavailing regrets—Reach the South American coast—Pernambuco—The surf breaking there—A hot residence—Catamarans—Proceeding southwards—Maceio—Flowers and scenery—Absence of bird-life—Flying-fish numerous—Fight between a whale and a swordfish—Rio de Janeiro—Santos—Hotbed of yellow fever—Everything in the wrong place—Sailor's philosophy—Quarantine station—Visit of health officer—Good-bye—Land at Montevideo—Kind reception by old friends 9-21

CHAPTER III

URUGUAY

Republic of Uruguay, or Banda Oriental del Uruguay—Smallest South American Republic—Area—Population—Compared with British, Dutch, and French Guiana—Geographical position—Greatest length and width—Boundaries—Face of the country—The Rio de la Plata little affected by tides—Salto Grande rapids—Rivers—Great floods—Geological features—Minerals—Montevideo—The bay—Proposed harbour and docks . 22-32

CHAPTER IV

EL PASO DE LOS TOROS

Northern terminus of the Central Uruguay Railway—Extension to Brazilian frontier—Multiplicity of names—Hard on patron saints—Picturesque spots on the Rio Negro—Resemblance to the Erne—My native river—Fish and birds—"Come back to Erin"—Crimson-flowering acacias—Cina-cina—Variety of water-fowl—Not long since beasts of prey roamed about here—A comfortable hotel—Watch-dog—Soothing him with the bagpipes—Afraid of a fox—Character for courage lost—Procuring fowl for table—"Aunt Sally"—Frequenters of the place—Bloodshed viewed with little concern—Object-lesson of hardening effects upon children—Get into trouble driving bullocks—"*Pulperias*"—A festive magistrate—In the "lock-up" 33-45

CHAPTER V

EXAMINING THE COUNTRY

PAGE

Began surveying operations—An uncomfortable night—Hard camping ground—Bed and bedding left behind—Tarantulas and scorpions—*Campo Santo*—Ostriches and deer—A polite host—Had to leave—Pressing business—Two ways of looking at the crime of murder—The upas-tree—Other superstitions—Cures—Dangerous to ride a grey horse in a thunderstorm—The river Tacuarembó Chico—Beautiful trees and flowers—Wild birds—Horses in the river Tres Cruces—Tres Cerros—Curiously shaped hills—Crossed the Tacuarembó Grande—Gold mines of Cuñapiru and Corrales—Lack of enthusiasm—Unpleasant reminiscences of a gold mine—Early visitors—A town of many "first officials" . . 46-63

CHAPTER VI

THE HAUNT OF THE OUTLAW

The Tambores valley—A steep ascent—Cactus plants—Parley with an attacking party—Explanations—Man robbed of his wife—Bereaved husband—Passing through the valley—A doubtful military protection—Where ignorance is bliss—Resting peacefully among the cut-throats—A lovely spot—Ruthless navvies—The soldiers we saw in the valley—Anticipate events—Special police force—Not much use—Outlaws troublesome—Matters get worse—The navvies solve the problem in their own way—They have a Sunday's shooting in the woods—Somewhat reticent about the bag they made—Dead men tell tales—Tambores afterwards less popular with outlaws—They migrate—Cattle farmer's escape—Second migration—Night attack upon a farmer's house—Robber killed by his companions—A victor on the field of bloodless battle—Nearly shooting by mistake—The workmen had their own little differences—Too many graves—"Valley of Eden"—The "Robber's Rest" 64–81

CHAPTER VII

WATCHMEN

Watchman, what of the night?—Discrepancies in information—A citizen's perplexities—The people of El Paso de los Toros—Reputation of the place—Accidental discharge of firearms—Walls of houses bullet-marked—A tragic occurrence—The knife did its work silently—The public uneasy—Watchmen appointed—Men of excellent character—Paraded and reviewed—Their first night on duty—A personal confession—Rumours that the watchmen slept on their posts—The chief of police tests the matter—Capture of lanterns—Explanations—Death-blow to the force—Our private watchmen—A New Year's visit—Shooting at a police-sergeant—Culprit caught and flogged—Private differences—Burglar fired at, but escaped 82–93

CHAPTER VIII

POLICE

Objections to police—Burglars dislike bulldogs—Personal experience of police—Effective assistance rendered by them—Timely information—Headquarters—Our office—Obliged to be careful—Gangs of robbers—A projected attack thwarted—The chief of police—Another attempt at burglary—Bringing money from the bank—Paying along the line—A friendly publican—Pay trains—Attempt to wreck a train 94–105

CHAPTER IX

PERILS BY LAND AND WATER

PAGE

A tour of inspection—Coach upset—Floundering in the mud —Rescued and washed down—A night at a wayside inn —Aggressive cats—Upsets not uncommon—Four falls in one day—A broken nose—Surgical skill—Professional jealousy—The rustic waits for the river to flow past— Horace and Tennyson not acquainted with South American rivers—A daily experience—Sudden floods and equally rapid subsidence—Flood in the Tacuarembó Chico—Search for a lost child—Floods in the Rio Negro —Many houses submerged—Upset in a flooded river— Rescued—Another disaster—Horse drowned—Many accidents crossing rivers—Two of them had fatal endings 106–119

CHAPTER X

LANDOWNERS, WORKMEN, ETC.

Landowners — Local information — Natural aptitude for selecting railway lines—Resemblance to hen lapwings —Different characters—A fierce landlord—A cold reception—A warning to trespassers—A sharp look-out— The wheel of fortune—An enemy converted into a friend —A generous offer—Unable to accept it—Difficulty of establishing a menagerie at a country house in Ireland —Another angry landlord—Surveyors' troubles—Saint Patrick's day—A special train asked for—A night attack—A general engagement—Killed, wounded, and prisoners—Disputed boundaries—Another class of landowners—Workmen—Italians—Austrians—Bavarians— Basques—Natives of Uruguay—Occasional troubles— Strikes—Outbreak of smallpox 120–133

CHAPTER XI

LITERA SCRIPTA MANET

PAGE

A general assertion nearly as often wrong as right—A maxim dear to members of the legal profession—Like Mesopotamia to the good old lady—The one safe anchorage upon the lawyer's chart—On a par with the arithmetical dogma that 2 and 2 make 4—The written letter flies away—Wafted up to the heavens—The reader's sympathy is sought—Unanswered letters—Letters found in a river—Stolen correspondence—A stolen despatch-box recovered—Missing title-deeds—Title-deeds rescued from being sold for waste paper—Pages cut out of manuscript records—Gravestones injured—Love-letters alone survive—After all, the maxim may have a different meaning 134–143

CHAPTER XII

SAN FRUCTUOSO

San Fructuoso or Tacuarembó—Approach to it—Houses and gardens—Public square—Australian trees—Promenades on summer evenings—A peculiar custom—The theatre—Enterprising inhabitants—Robbers in the suburbs—A row upon the river—Foliage, flowers, and birds—"The Fern Grotto"—Tree-ferns—Soothing effect—A lovely spot—Nature's pictures 144–154

CHAPTER XIII

IN THE GARDEN

Enjoyable half-hours—The sunflower—Mistake of the poets—Professors of æsthetic art—Blind leaders of the blind—Lily of the Nile—A less thirsty flower—The Scarborough lily—Beautiful flowers—Black ants—Their red relations—Warfare—Ant-hills on bedroom floor—Hard to appease—Humming-birds—Oven-birds—Their nests—Peculiar strut—Advantage of the form of nest—An unwelcome visitor—"Not at home"—New tenants—The South American swallow—The garden in the night-time—Frogs of various kinds — Their concerts and oratory—The *clepsydra*—The brown stork—Its dreadful voice—Mystery explained 155–167

CHAPTER XIV

THE FOUR-LEAFED SHAMROCK

The minstrel's song—The magic plant—How I found it—Awaiting extra good fortune—In a state of perpetual suspense, like Sidney Smith's young clergyman—Other trefoils—The midwinter primrose—Winter—The heart-marked trefoil—Better emblem for Ireland—A pity Saint Patrick was in such a hurry—Irishmen, whether saints or sinners, are inclined to be impulsive—Saint Patrick's nationality—Particulars of his early life and history—Claims of the Scots and Gauls—A case of *non sequitur*—A fly in amber—Intercourse between Ireland and Gaul—A county Wexford man became Roman emperor—Soldiers of fortune—Did Saint Patrick banish snakes and toads from Scotland and Gaul, as he did from Ireland? 168–174

CHAPTER XV

THE SNAKE IN THE GRASS

Latet anguis in herbâ—Good serpentine society—They don't appear to wish for concealment—One meets with them in the most unexpected places—Visit from a snake and toad while in my bath—An Irishman to the rescue—Catches the toad with a lasso—The lasso used for all purposes—Snakes eat toads—Dog and snake story—Snakes in numbers—Flooded out—Snakes on the railway—Lost no man from snake bites, and but one from the bite of a toad—"A frog bit him" . . . 175–180

CHAPTER XVI

LAW AND LAWYERS

Why bandage the eyes of Justice?—Legal "blind man's buff"—A wide field for investigation—Too great a growth of lawyers—Personal experience—Peculiar people—Many excellent men—Legal troubles with contractor—A part greater than the whole!—Euclid at fault—Judge taxed with corruption—Contempt of court not in force—Overtures for a settlement—What came of them—Lawyer and client—Attempt to rob a farmer—An attorney-general shot—Newspaper comments on the occurrence—Land arbitration extraordinary—Legal partition of property leaving out the heirs—Coffee with the chief—Something up—Half a loaf better than no bread—Sleeping Justice suddenly awakes—Eviction on a wholesale scale—A judge in gaol . . . 181–191

CHAPTER XVII

AMATEUR DIPLOMACY

One never knows what he can do till he tries—Unskilled in the ways of the "foreign office"—A diplomatic difficulty—Home-made measures—Immense dissatisfaction—Overtures of peace—Conditions accepted and acted upon—Another diplomatic difficulty—A Christmas dinner—The loan of a band—International etiquette—The toasts—Her Majesty's health—Preliminary protest—Objections overcome in the end—"God save the Queen"—Great enthusiasm—The President's health—Good feeling restored—All's well that ends well—A diplomatist's doubts 192–201

CHAPTER XVIII

PEN VERSUS SWORD

PAGE

"The pen is mightier than the sword"—The editor who got 309 lashes—"There's luck in odd numbers"—The stout editor in trouble—*In mĕdio tutissimus ibis*—Adding insult to injury—A rare job for the tailor—A worse fate—A fierce colonel—Twelve thousand lashes!—Unceremonious burial—"The Bold Soldier Boy"—Mickey Free—The South American "Tommy Atkins"—The colonel under a cloud—His explanation—Much force in it—Recruiting from the gaols—Something to be said on the other side—Leniency towards criminals—Keeping their hands in practice—The editor flushed with victory—Sufficiently outspoken—Meets an opponent—Contest of smallarms—No one hurt except a stray dog—Editor leaves, finding the place unhealthy—A government official attacked and severely wounded—One of his antagonists caught—Nothing comes of it . 202-210

CHAPTER XIX

RIVERA AND SANTA ANA

A town of many "first officials"—Twin towns—Neutral zone—High hills—Source of the river Cuñapiru—Population—Toll-keeper and his wife—Mr. Weller's theory only partly borne out—Most hospitable people—Cherry-brandy unsuited to a warm climate—Escape from a dilemma—Chief trade—Shooting contrabandists—"Under the poncho"—An attractive spot—A young jaguar—Santa Ana—Wants a custom-house—Accident to an engineer—A Brazilian surgeon—An unpleasant suggestion—A consultation—Narrow escape from suffocation—Fancy method for getting clear of mosquitoes—Life upon the frontier—Exponents of "free trade"—Reports of firearms in the night-time—Double supply of amusement—

A *feu de joie*—Excess of zeal—Neutral zone again—The troubles of a photographer—Blackmail levied on hotel-keepers—Brazilian doctor has to fly . . . 211–221

CHAPTER XX

IN REVOLUTIONARY TIMES

Prevalence of revolutions—Like "whirlwinds"—First experience of the kind—Pure patriotism—Out of office and in office—Political "beggar my neighbour"—A perennial subject of discussion—Safety of the state—Officially communicated—Invitation to witness a battle—Explanations—The battle—Terrific firing—No one hurt—Capitulation—Sacrifice of self-interest—Laying down arms—An open secret—A traitor in the camp—Convinces all but one—The plot thickens—A banquet in barracks—Guests arrive—Betrayed—Bloodshed in the banqueting-hall—Arresting political opponents—Honourable conduct of a government official—A train captured by insurgents—Soldiers put to death—Living on the enemy—A military receipt—Opportunities for revenge—A nice discrimination between methods of killing—Man with his hands cut off—His end—Evils arising from the revolutionary spirit—Injury to credit and prosperity 222–237

CHAPTER XXI

NATURAL HISTORY NOTES

Larger wild animals disappearing—Wild-cats and foxes still numerous—Deer of two kinds—Armadilloes—Anteater—Carpinchoes—Nutrias—Otters—Freshwater seals—Eagles of three kinds: blue, brown, and black—Hawks—Vultures—Falcons—Game-birds—*Pavo del Monte*—Man shot by a bird—Partridges of two kinds—Snaring partridges—Shooting snipe over a bull-terrier

—A sporting pig—The giant stork—Ordinary storks—
A pet stork—A strange bird—The brown stork—My
aviary—Other pets—A coati—Tame tortoise—One of
Nature's gentlemen 238-254

CHAPTER XXII

CLIMATE OF URUGUAY

Hot in summer, but climate good and healthy—Mr. Mulhall's Handbook, and statistics as to heat and cold, &c.
—Our register of same—The seasons—Dust storms—
Curious experiences—Dust storms followed by heavy
rain—Lightning—Large hailstones—Locusts—Stopping trains—Difficulty of keeping cool in summer—
Various suggestions—A new plan to prevent one's
"head swelling"—The Dead March in Saul, with variations—Improving upon orders—A good shaking up—
Meteorites 255-265

CHAPTER XXIII

RAILWAYS OF URUGUAY

Railways essential to the progress of the country—No public
roads worthy of the name—Former means of communication—Wire fencing—Road allowances—Advantages
of carriage by rail—Railways begun in 1867—Durazno
line the first one started—Its subsequent progress—
Central Uruguay Railway—The Pando Railway—Frequent change of name—The Central Uruguay Eastern
Extension—The Central Uruguay Northern Extension—
Uruguay Great Eastern—Midland Railway—North-
Western Railway—Northern Railway—Projected
Western Railway—Railway from Montevideo to the
slaughter yards—Best policy with regard to railways
—Railway mania in Argentina—Growth and present
extent of railways in Uruguay 266-276

CHAPTER XXIV

CONCLUSION

Rôle of candid friend—Skeletons in cupboards—You can't hide them—They should be banished—The persons reflected upon do not represent society generally—Their misdeeds are condemned—The wants of South American States—Strong and just governments—Requires no great sacrifice or self-denial—The people of the River Plate—Kindly feeling—Willing testimony regarding them—A bright and prosperous region if only the demon of political revolution were exorcised and banished . 277–280

SOUTH AMERICAN SKETCHES

CHAPTER I

INTRODUCTION

WE are frequently told by people with a didactic turn of mind, that it is always the unexpected that happens. They appear to think that by conveying their wisdom in epigrammatic form, just as chemists encase the nauseous ingredients of their pills in a coating of some less disagreeable substance, the mental palate may be deceived into accepting the proffered instruction without remonstrance.

Critics may suggest that it is only another way of saying we don't possess the gift of prophecy; but that if we were more careful to note what is going on around us, we should find events turning out in accordance with our anticipations much oftener than they now appear to do.

However this may be, I think most people will agree with me in assuming that unanticipated events do occur with sufficient frequency to give the assertion a popular currency, even though such coincidences may fail to establish a fixed law in the matter; just as a light sovereign may remain in general circulation, and be accepted as if retaining its full weight and value, when deficient in both.

For my own part, the unexpected has so frequently occurred to me, that scarcely anything would surprise me now. I will mention one instance of the kind, which I think should suffice to convince those sceptical about the matter.

Towards the close of the year 1888 I went to London, and upon arriving there I was handed a telegram that had reached my home in Ireland after my departure from thence, and had been sent on to me. It contained a request that I should come over to have an interview with some gentlemen in the city upon a subject about which they wished to speak with me.

When I had breakfasted I called upon the sender of the telegram, who expressed much surprise at the rapidity with which I made my appearance in response to his communication. My explanations, however, corrected the somewhat too hasty conclusion at which he had arrived as to the speed attainable by the modern appliances of travel in these islands, and we proceeded to business.

It related to a project for the construction of a railway in Uruguay, which the gentlemen interested in it were anxious I should carry out, and after some negotiation I agreed to do so.

I think this may be accepted as a fair example of the unexpected happening, for when I left home I had no more intention of going to the River Plate again, than I had of embarking on a voyage of discovery to the North Pole.

In the following pages we are about to visit a country upon the other side of the globe, where everything presents opposite characteristics to what we are accustomed to observe in their equivalents at home. The inhabitants stand with their heads pointing downwards, and their feet directed upwards towards ours; the sun is in the north at noon; and midsummer occurs at Christmastide. These, and many other interesting peculiarities, combine to impress upon the traveller in Uruguay the feeling that he is in a strange land of curious phenomena, if not quite in such an enchanted region as that so charmingly described in "Through the Looking-Glass."

Under inverted circumstances of the kind, it may well be permitted to one who essays to sketch some of the peculiar features of the country and of its people, to depart from the time-honoured custom of placing the moral to be conveyed at the end of the narrative, and to establish a new precedent by opening with it, as a fit introduction to what is to follow.

There is a manifest advantage in this treatment of the subject, for the unwary reader is thus ensnared in the meshes of the moral, to his own great benefit, before he is aware of the fact. Whereas, when the moral comes at the end, the majority of readers having by that time had their curiosity satiated, pass over it unread, and cast the book aside, just as a schoolboy, when he has sucked an orange dry, throws away the rind, as unworthy of his further attention.

To prevent any such mishap in the present instance, I will state, without further circumlocution, that the lesson I wish to convey at the start is the desirability of cultivating a habit of civility and politeness in our intercourse with our fellow-men. In order to impress this the more forcibly upon the minds of my readers, I shall proceed to illustrate the benefits arising from a strict adherence to the principles of the maxim I have laid down.

While engaged in making preparations for my departure to South America, I had frequent interviews with the officials of the steamship company by whose line we proposed to make the voyage, and found them to be most reasonable and obliging; and in consequence of the manner in which suggestions of mine had been met by the directors, I wrote to thank them for it. Some days afterwards, having occasion to visit the office again, their representative said he wanted to introduce me to the directors, who were then sitting at a board meeting. "I don't mind telling you," he added, "that you are the first person who ever wrote them a civil letter, and they are anxious to make the acquaintance of one who has afforded them such an unusual experience."

Thus it happened that I was introduced in the character of the civil letter writer.

I was not a little amused by the incident, and thought the matter had ended there; but this was by no means the case. Just before sailing I received a letter from the secretary of the company, enclosing an introduction to the captain of the ship in which our passages were taken. It was unsolicited on my part, and unexpected; and was, moreover, an official document, written by order of the directors, to request that every attention should be paid to me, and to the staff of engineers accompanying me, so as to make the voyage as agreeable as possible for us.

Upon 22nd November 1888, the day of our departure, we went on board, and seeing that the captain was much occupied at first with the affairs of the ship, I postponed presenting my letter of introduction until a more favourable opportunity. This I found later in the evening, after we had dropped the pilot, and when the captain was enjoying a cigar, as he paced the quarter-deck. He read the secretary's letter with an amused expression on his face, and then, laughingly, asked me how I had managed to make the directors take such a special interest in me. He had himself, he said, received a strongly worded private letter from the secretary to much the same effect as the official one I gave him; in addition to which, about an hour before sailing, a telegraphic reminder, of similar import, had reached him. I told him the story of the civil letter, which he heartily enjoyed.

Here I may state that he fully carried out his instructions with regard to us, and moreover, that he was a most agreeable and well-read man, whose information was not bounded by a nautical horizon, but extended far beyond it into a wide expanse of general knowledge.

This incident of the civil letter and its results go far to prove the correctness of my contention on the subject of politeness, and to remove the erroneous impression so widely current, that directors of companies are impervious to ordinary civility, or indeed to everything but abuse.

Some of the less charitably-minded of my acquaintances may, possibly, fancy that I have another, and personal, motive for being so communicative about this trivial matter, and that I am actuated by a desire to obtain for myself an indirect certificate of character for urbanity in the capacity of a letter writer, a quality they may think not always characteristic of my style.

To such I would reply that they are illogical in their deductions, arguing from a particular to a general case, when they infer from some rare specimen of my correspondence what the general law is that regulates it.

In one's dealings with the world it is not always possible to set everything right by the simple remedy of *suaviter in modo*, as if it were one of those patent medicines which are warranted to cure all complaints. Obstinate cases, showing a tendency to assume a chronic character, are sometimes to be met with, to combat which it becomes necessary to have recourse to the stronger expedient of *fortiter in re*. Under these circumstances, it will be readily understood that the hand of even a much more skilful compounder than I can claim to be may occasionally shake a little when making up the *recipe*, and add, perhaps, a drop too much of the stronger ingredient to the mixture, giving it a more bitter taste than it was intended it should have.

CHAPTER II

"A LIFE ON THE OCEAN WAVE"

THE voyage began pleasantly enough. Everything was in our favour; the weather and the sea were alike propitious as we ran down the Channel and across the Bay of Biscay. On the third day out we called at Carril and Vigo, ports, or rather indentations, of the western coast of Spain, about thirty miles apart. The towns themselves are picturesquely situated on sloping hill sides, shut in by a background of mountains. At each of them we embarked about 150 Basque emigrants for the River Plate. As far as the male portion of these was concerned, the Spanish officials examined their passports and certificates of military service with great care and minuteness, to prevent any one escaping from the country without having fulfilled his duty in this respect.

The officials themselves seemed very proud of a singularly long finger-nail on each of their

hands, as bearing evidence that their grade in the social scale was above that employed in manual labour. To such an extent does the custom pervade Spanish society, that it is no uncommon thing to see men very little raised above the labouring classes assiduously cultivating a distinctive peculiarity of the kind.

From Vigo we made for Lisbon, where we added to the number of people on board a good many steerage passengers of Portuguese nationality, bound for Brazil. Proceeding next to Saint Vincent we took in a supply of coal there, and then steered across the Atlantic.

Here we may pause for a while, to pay some attention to those on board, among whom were an old acquaintance of mine and his wife, going out for a trip to the River Plate, and their agreeable society added greatly to the pleasantness of the voyage.

We were singularly fortunate in our fellow-passengers, many of whom proved to be interesting companions, while some of them were conspicuous in contributing to what I may term the social success of our life at sea.

There was a little Brazilian gentleman, who

bestirred himself to the utmost to provide amusement of various kinds for all his fellow-passengers, whose entertainment he took under his own special care. In fact, he appeared almost offended if any one was discovered comfortably ensconced in some quiet spot on deck, reading an interesting book, and enjoying in peace and quietness the delicious sea-breeze. It was a slight to his powers as a caterer for the general amusement that any one should prefer an occupation other than that which he had provided, knowing it to be most suitable and best for the occasion. He was full of expedients for killing time. He was even a sort of variety show in himself, and would have made an excellent actor on the theatrical stage, for Nature had given him a face as mobile as his character. In a moment he could change the expression of his features from a realistic representation of the depths of misery, into which he had been plunged by his remorseless and only enemy, sea-sickness, to a facial arrangement suggestive of the most perfect concentration of light-hearted and mischievous fun. He knew something of all the modern languages of Europe, though his knowledge of them was not profound, and his application of it occasionally suggested the inference that his education in foreign tongues had been acquired rather in the byways than the highways of learning.

It was most amusing to hear him explaining to some unimpressionable person the fascinations and allurements of a game at "poker," or of a sweepstake on the ship's daily run. One could almost fancy that, to him, life, without some such excitement, would suggest an imperfect, colourless, and unenjoyable existence.

There were many others among the passengers well deserving of a favourable notice, but to describe them all is quite impossible.

There was one, however, upon whom not to bestow a word or two of appreciative recognition would stamp me as being devoid of all æsthetic perceptions. This was a lady, beside whom it was my good fortune to be placed at table. The advantageous position thus acquired was not of my own seeking. It was the steward who put me there, and thus brought down upon me the envious feelings of several young gentlemen, who scarcely concealed how much they desired to change places with me.

The lady I refer to possessed among other attractions a great mass of beautiful golden hair; none of those artificial productions, the creation of "auricomus fluid," but the real genuine growth, that Nature alone could supply in such burnished brilliancy. It made a glowing halo around the head it decked, like that of some mediæval saint, suggestive of a shrine, at which, as already hinted, it was easy to see there were several of the passengers prepared to worship.

But here I must check my too erratic pen, which, having got upon this subject, seems well disposed to ramble on, forgetful of the fact that feminine beauty and attractions must be reserved for poets to describe, the cold and harsh reality of prose being wholly unfitted for the purpose. Besides, the subject is an exceedingly delicate one to deal with. Who can tell whether the violet would not much rather be left to exhale its fragrance unperceived beneath the shade of its protecting leaves, than to be brought forth from its seclusion into the glare of public notice and admiration?

As I sat beside the centre of attraction I could not be ignorant of the fact that, however great might be the advantages of my position, it was not without its drawbacks; just as philosophers tell us there is no cup of happiness, however full, that does not contain some bitter ingredient. There were my rivals, all attention, with ears strained to catch even fragmentary portions of my feeble attempts to be agreeable to my fascinating neighbour; while adverse criticism of the performance was stereotyped upon their faces beforehand, and shone from unfriendly eyes with the green light of jealousy.

No one shall ever know, if I can help it, the mental torture I endured while passing through that trying ordeal; or how deeply I regretted my former folly in neglecting to master the details of that useful volume, "Principles of the Art of Conversation," by my friend Professor M———, a competent knowledge of which is in itself a liberal education. Had I but assimilated even a small portion of its wisdom, I could not have gone astray. But under the trying circumstances of my position, the knowledge intended to be conveyed in the professor's pages deserted me completely. I remembered, it is true, that it forbids, under heavy penalties, any reference to the weather, or other common topic, when addressing a new acquaintance; and suggests the most prudent course to pursue in order to ingratiate yourself with an elderly lady afflicted with numerous children, or a young one blessed with none. But not a single hint, or even word, could I recall to guide me how to act in the absence of any definite information as to these family matters, when conversing with an attractive lady possessing a wealth of golden hair.

It is useless, however, wasting time in vain regrets over what might have been, and in lamenting lost opportunities; so we had better proceed upon the voyage, about which there is little to report.

Upon December 7th we reached the South American coast at Pernambuco, where the sea was breaking over a ledge of rocks in front of the town with sufficient fury to strike terror into the hearts of sailors as well as of landsmen. Behind the ledge, however, there was a bay of smooth water, in which small coasting craft could lie securely, if their navigators knew the entrance to it. A castaway captain with whom I once travelled told me that his ship was burnt at sea, and he and his crew had to take to an open boat, in which they reached Pernambuco after sailing 400 miles. But so frightened were his men when they saw the surf breaking on the shore, that they wanted him to put about and make for some other port, notwithstanding that they were in a most wretched condition.

Pernambuco is an extremely hot residence in summer, and the red-tiled roofs of the houses intensify the effect of the heat, as far as appearance goes. The land lies low along the coast, except at the point called Lindah, an early Portuguese settlement, where it is hilly.

It is on the higher background that the houses of the principal merchants are built, among mango groves, bananas, and palm-trees, surrounded on all sides by luxuriant tropical vegetation, including orchids innumerable.

The fishing catamarans that passed our ship as she lay at anchor formed a curious feature in the scene before us. They are generally constructed of six pieces of rounded timber, placed longitudinally parallel to each other, and close together, a couple of cross-pieces, to which they are bound, keeping them in their proper position.

The raft thus formed is furnished with a rough board seat, placed aft for the convenience of the helmsman, who is also captain, cook, and crew; and on this he sits in a fairly dry position as regards his body, while the water rushes up between the timbers of the raft and washes his feet. The sail with which a catamaran is usually furnished has the appearance of a triangle with curved sides. The mast is bent like a fishing-rod when playing a fish, and a "sprit," projecting from it at right angles, takes the place of a boom, keeping the lower part of the sail stretched. Such sails appeared to be only used for running before the wind, so that if this is the case, the raft must be propelled by oars when it is desired to go to windward.

When the passengers and cargo for Pernambuco had been landed, our ship weighed anchor and proceeded southward, at a distance of some three or four miles from the coast. This for the most part presented the appearance of low sand-hills, with a fringe of palm-trees at their base.

On the following day we touched at Maceio, where the foreshore was low, and consisted of a white sandy beach, palm-trees growing everywhere, almost down to the seaside. The land rose to a considerably higher level at no great distance from the shore, while the water in the bay was beautifully clear, and of a bright green colour. Some of the passengers who went on shore brought back lovely flowers and large bunches of the gaudy-coloured *bougainvillea*.

From Maceio we made for Bahia, the character of the coast-line remaining much the same as on our course the previous day. The weather was glorious, with a cloudless sky overhead, while the water beneath for many miles was of a deep shade of ultramarine, the whole forming a perfect picture of tropical coast-scenery. One peculiarity I remarked about it, and that not for the first time, was the strange absence of bird life at this particular part of our voyage, although there were plenty of flying fish to furnish food for them.

At this same place, upon another trip, I witnessed a fight between a whale and a swordfish, which lasted for a considerable time. During the encounter the whale kept part of its body above water, the surface of which it lashed into spray with the furious beating of its tail. We did not see the ending of the duel, but the captain told us a fight of the kind usually terminates in favour of the swordfish.

The remaining ports that we called at were Bahia, Rio de Janeiro, and Santos, from which latter place we were glad to get away, owing to the evil reputation it bears, in a sanitary point of view, as a "hot-bed" for propagating yellow fever. Nor can one wonder at this, for the ill-smelling ooze and slime along the foreshore are just of the class to fester into noxious gases under a scorching sun.

There was nothing to note about the rest of our voyage; in fact, from first to last, the only remarkable thing about it was that, as regards the sea itself, we had everything in the wrong place. In northern latitudes, where we looked for rough water, we found it calm and smooth, whereas, when we steamed southwards into a region where the ocean is generally tranquil and at rest, it was nearly all the time disturbed and "choppy," although no corresponding wind existed to account for its roughness. The only explanation of this which was given us by those on board, who were learned in the habits and customs of the sea, was that it must have been blowing hard somewhere else. I thought this philosophy had much to recommend its general adoption in matters unexplainable, and I hoped to comfort myself thereafter by a similar process of reasoning about many things I do not understand. It is so pleasant to think, with the honest, simple-minded mariner, that every effect must have had a cause of some kind to produce it, and it is useless to go on puzzling our brains further about the matter.

After a run of twenty-six days, ending a week before Christmas, we reached Flores Island, the quarantine station for Uruguay. It was a miserable place, and its buildings and appointments gave it a most depressing aspect. When the health officers came alongside and received the report of the surgeon of the ship, there was a long consultation as to whether we should be allowed to land at Montevideo, which was our destination, or be compelled to spend a probationary time in quarantine, as some of the ports our ship had touched at were declared to be infected.

In the end, after considerable deliberation, the

authorities, to our great satisfaction, decided upon adopting the former course. So, when we had said good-bye to those on board, we passed down the gangway to a little steamer full of old friends, who had come out to meet me, and from whom the kindly greetings I received on all sides were of the warmest and most flattering kind. Then with three loud cheers from us for those we were leaving, responded to energetically from the ship, we cast off and made for the shore, where a reception no less warm and kindly from other friends awaited me.

CHAPTER III

URUGUAY

BEFORE proceeding further it is desirable that the general reader should be made acquainted with the main features of the country to which he has been brought, and where it is proposed to detain him during his stay in South America.

But though Uruguay may be his temporary home, he will be taken, in thought, from time to time to witness occurrences in other portions of that great continent.

The Republic of Uruguay, or the "Banda Oriental del Uruguay" as it is formally styled, and still shorter, colloquially, as the "Banda Oriental," is the smallest of South American Republics, of which there are ten, besides three colonies, the latter belonging respectively to England, France, and Holland.

It has an area of 73,000 square miles, or rather more than four-fifths of that of Great Britain.

Uruguay occupies about one per cent. of the surface of South America, and has about two per cent. of its population, or say, 750,000 persons.

It is about two-thirds of the size of British Guiana, one-half larger than Dutch Guiana, and three times the size of French Guiana.

Uruguay lies on the north-eastern or left bank of the Rio de la Plata, between the parallels of 30° 5' and 35° south latitude, and 53° and 58° 20' west longitude.

Its greatest length is about 360 miles, measured in a straight line north-west by north, from Maldonado on its southern or Atlantic coast, to the river Cuareim.

The maximum width is about 310 miles, from Palmeira, on the river Uruguay, to the Laguna Mirim, a little to the east of Artigas, which direction cuts the line of greatest length at nearly right angles, at a distance of some ninety miles from the sea coast.

Boundaries.—Uruguay is bounded on the north and north-east by Brazil, from which it is separated in part by the rivers Cuareim and Jaguaron, falling respectively into the river Uruguay and the Laguna Mirim, the remaining portion of the northern boundary being a frontier land line joining the waters of the two rivers above mentioned.

The rest of the eastern boundary is formed by the Laguna Mirim and the Atlantic Ocean, which latter, and the Rio de la Plata, constitute the southern boundary. On the west, Uruguay is bounded by the river of the same name, which separates it from the Argentine Confederation.

Face of the Country.—The surface of Uruguay differs altogether from the very level character of the Pampas formation in Buenos Ayres, on the Argentine, or southern side of the Rio de la Plata.

A special feature of the land is the number of main ridges or water-sheds running in different directions and sending out lateral spurs, so that the general character of the country, especially towards the north, is a combination of hills, valleys, and rolling plains.

Uruguay, although generally inferior to Argentina as regards the quality of its soil for agricultural purposes, and unable to support an equal head of cattle for the same area, has many advantages of its own. The tortuous sequence of hills and valleys affords shelter to cattle and sheep, no matter from what point of the compass a gale may blow; while the permanent rivers, with which the country is so well watered, relieve the farmers from the great anxiety and labour that fall to the lot of their southern neighbours, in consequence of the shrinking of the streams during droughts.

Rivers.—The first and most important of these—the Rio de la Plata—is, strictly speaking, not a single river, but the channel through which the waters of a collection of rivers—the Parana, Uruguay, Paraguay, and their tributaries—are conveyed to and discharged into the sea. It is assumed to begin at the junction of the rivers Parana and Uruguay, and has a course of 150 miles from that point to the Atlantic, if we take the configuration of the coast-line as determining its extent. Seafaring men, however, consider it to flow for some distance farther into the ocean, in consequence of the prevailing freshness of the water in the locality.

Though so comparatively short, it should be remembered that the Rio de la Plata is in reality the name given to what is only the lower reach of a river system, the central artery of which has a continuous course of not far short of 2500 miles.

It is to be observed that the Rio de la Plata is little affected by ordinary tides; but being about 60 miles wide at its mouth, and less than half that width 120 miles higher up its course, it presents what may be termed a funnel-shaped estuary, in which the water is frequently banked up to a considerable height by strong winds blowing up the channel.

The next river in importance is the Uruguay, which gives its name to the country we are dealing with, and forms, as we have seen, a portion of its boundary.

After an independent course of about 1000 miles it joins the Parana and loses its identity.

Although a majestic river, it is only navigable by moderate sized ocean-going steamers for the lower forty miles of its course or thereabouts. Smaller craft, drawing from six to eight feet, can, however, ascend it for 200 miles, to the rapids known as the *Salto Grande* (or Great Leap), situated about twelve miles above the town of Salto, an important centre of population on the left bank of the river.

A specially constructed steamer, drawing very little water, used at one time to be poled and warped past this obstruction up a narrow channel in the rapids, along their right or Argentine bank. Once above this point the river, though shallow in many places, is navigable for small vessels up to and beyond the frontier of Brazil.

Some years ago, while engaged in making the survey for a canal to overcome these rapids, which it was contemplated at the time to construct as a Government work, I ascended the river as far as the town of Uruguayana, in Brazil, taking soundings all the way, and finding it to be as I have described; but the project was not carried out.

The foregoing remarks as to the available depth of water in the river Uruguay apply to its normal state only, as it is subject to great floods, completely altering the aspect of the navigation.

There is another class of rivers to be dealt with, consisting of those which intersect the country. Of these by far the most important is the Rio Negro, which takes its rise in Brazil, and after running in a south-westerly direction through the heart of Uruguay for a distance of more than 300 miles, joins the river Uruguay at about latitude 33° 20′ south. Like the river into which it flows, it is also subject to great floods. The Rio Negro divides the country into two parts of unequal size, the northern portion being considerably smaller, less fertile, and more broken, rugged, and thinly populated than that lying to the south of it. The scanty nature of the population may be partially accounted for by the absence of roads and the want of bridges; but these are disadvantages which railways will gradually neutralise.

The river Yi is an important affluent of the Rio Negro, into which also flow the waters of the Cuñapiru, the Tacuarembó Grande and Chico, the Rubio Chico, and Tres Cruces. The Cuareim, as already mentioned, forms part of the northern frontier with Brazil, and empties itself into the Uruguay, as do also the Arapey, Dayman, and Queguay. The Santa Lucia falls into the Rio de la Plata a little to the west of Montevideo, while the Cebollati discharges itself into the Laguna Mirim, which forms part of the eastern boundary of the country.

These are the chief rivers of Uruguay, and they are all subject to considerable floods during heavy rains.

Geological Features.—Rock of a granitic description prevails in the neighbourhood of Montevideo and in the south generally, affording excellent paving materials. Limestone is found to the south-east and in some parts of the interior.

Going northwards, a friable rock is met with, having the appearance of being formed from indurated clay, and exhibiting a peculiar curved fracture when broken up. This formation extends to some distance north of the Rio Negro, and then gives place to sandstone, the beds of which latter deposit furnish very fine building material.

To the north-east and north, near the Brazilian frontier, quartz occasionally appears, and in the former direction there are gold mines, but the working of them has not as yet been very profitable or encouraging.

Considerable deposits of gravel, containing agates, carnelian, and other pebbles, are not uncommon, and I have heard of one instance in which two diamonds were found among the gravel ballast used for the railway; but they were of no great intrinsic value.

By far the most interesting mineralogical specimens in Uruguay are, in my estimation, the so-called water-stones.

They are small, white, and transparent; hollow in the interior, and partially filled with water, so that a bubble of air moves about upon its surface, according to the position in which the object is held.

These stones consist of pure silex, their surface presenting the appearance of a series of little curves and nodules, all rounded and smoothed off, as if the material had once been in a viscous state, while the interior of the broken stones that I have seen exhibits a mass of crystalline structure principally made up of hexagonal prisms terminating in similar pyramids.

How have these stones been formed? That is a question about which geologists may differ, but I think that one stage of their production is easy enough to understand.

Water, impregnated with a considerable amount of silex, dripping through the crevices of a rock into a small cavity in it, would deposit crystals of silex upon the top, bottom, and sides of the cavity, the crystals all pointing inwards. This operation being continued through long periods might gradually form a complete external casing, and eventually close any aperture in it, leaving therein the water and air that it happened to contain at the time.

But how are we to account for the external appearance of these geological curiosities? Can the material of which the matrix consisted have had anything to say to it? These, and other questions that will suggest themselves to the inquirer, are interesting subjects for consideration, which had better, perhaps, be left to the treatment of experts.

Montevideo.—This is the capital of the Republic, its only city and principal port. It is well situated, about the middle point of the southern coast, at what may be roughly called the mouth of the Rio de la Plata, though, as has been already said, the water continues fresh for many miles farther out to sea.

Montevideo, including its suburbs, has about 250,000 inhabitants, that is to say, speaking approximately, it absorbs one-third of the entire population of the Republic. It is a well-built city, and some of the suburban houses, surrounded by gardens and pleasure grounds, are very attractive.

It is situated upon a promontory forming one side of a bay, the depth of water in which is, unfortunately, insufficient for shipping purposes, and this condition of affairs is aggravated by the fact that the bay is said to be silting up. Ocean-going steamers have to lie out at anchor in the open roadstead. Many proposals for establishing a properly constructed port, with docks, at Montevideo have been made from time to time for the last quarter of a century, but without practical effect. Recently, however, the matter seemed to have assumed a new and more promising phase; but the outbreak of a revolution pushed this very necessary work into the background, from which it is to be hoped it will be brought forward before long.

None of the other centres of population in Uruguay call for any special notice in a general description of the country, being merely places for supplying the wants of the surrounding districts.

CHAPTER IV

EL PASO DE LOS TOROS

THE work we were about to undertake was practically an extension of the Central Uruguay Railway, from its then northern terminus on the right bank of the Rio Negro, distant 170 miles from Montevideo, to the town of Rivera, at the frontier of Brazil, a farther length of about 182 miles.

Our starting-point possessed a multiplicity of names. It is generally known as the Paso de los Toros, but the railway people give it the shorter designation of Rio Negro, after the river flowing past it, while its legal name is, I believe, Santa Isabel.

A residence of some time there impressed me with the conviction that there are at least occasional mistakes made in assigning certain places to patron saints, for I feel sure that none such, if their wishes could be consulted, would accept the charge of the locality in question.

It would almost seem as if the manner of appointment of a patron saint was somewhat similar to that of the high sheriff of a county with us; the victim has no choice or option in the matter, and must act if appointed.

Call it by whatever name we may, it is not a place of much interest. It owes its origin to the existence of a ford in the river at that point, which is passable, however, only when the water is low, so that in former times, before the introduction of ferry-boats, which preceded railways, passengers arriving there in any other condition of the river were obliged to await upon its bank a more favourable opportunity for crossing over.

Although the Paso de los Toros is not in itself calculated to excite much admiration, there are many parts of the Rio Negro near it that are very picturesque. There is a lovely reach of it about a league below the town, that reminded me of a scene on my native river—the Erne—at a place called *Mois Rhua*, which Saxon anglers who frequent our shores have corrupted into the more easily pronounced but less poetic name of "Moss Row."

I have called it my native river, and I think I

am entitled to do so, for I was born on its bank, and got dipped in its waters, both purposely and accidentally, many times in my youth. Possibly it may be due to this early aqueous experience that the Erne has always been for me the standard of beauty with which to compare the scenery upon other rivers.

To return to the Rio Negro; when I first saw the part of it to which I have referred, large fish were jumping in it, making rings upon its surface, just as salmon would do of a summer's day with us at home. A solitary cormorant was swimming about as unconcernedly as if it were in the Erne, while kingfishers followed their usual calling, and rasped out an unmusical chuckle from time to time, when they succeeded in capturing something particularly choice.

Such were the general surroundings, which were of a nature to make me feel, if prone to indulge in day-dreams, that I had accepted the invitation in the song to "Come back to Erin," and had been wafted unconsciously to her shores by some magic process. But there were other matters to attract attention and correct all such erroneous impressions. Black-necked swans floated lazily about, while rose-coloured spoon-bills waded in the shallow water along the river's edge, stirring up the silt in search of food, and brown storks flitted awkwardly from tree to tree. These animated objects broke the spell woven by the similarity of the landscape to a familiar scene at home. —

In another locality the blossoms of a number of crimson-flowering acacias clustering together made a fine display of colour against a background of evergreen shrubs. The *cina-cina*, too, a tree of the Mimosa family, presented an opposition show of creamy-white flowers yielding a fragra t perfume.

In the vicinity there was a lake, the favourite haunt of a wonderful variety of wildfowl, some of them with brilliant plumage.

Not many years ago beasts of prey roamed about where the Paso de los Toros now stands. Within the memory of the present owner of the adjoining lands two jaguars were shot there in one day. Wild dogs were frequently to be met with, sometimes in formidable packs; but such conditions have become altogether matters of the past.

Those wild animals, that are dangerous to flocks

and herds, are fast disappearing before the increase of the latter, every expedient being resorted to by the settlers to extirpate them. Only very rarely are specimens of the kind still to be met with in Uruguay, and that in the most unfrequented and secluded places.

Upon our arrival at the Paso de los Toros we took up our temporary residence, until permanent arrangements could be made, at a comfortable hotel which the Central Uruguay Railway Company had built for the convenience of travellers. One thing about it which struck me as peculiar was the great precaution that was taken to prevent burglars entering by the back of the house, while the front was left to take care of itself.

The back of the building opened upon a terrace, to which access from the yard below was obtained by a flight of stone steps. Parallel, and close to the outer edge of this terrace, and stretching the whole length of it, was an overhead wire rope, upon which worked a running ring, with a long chain and dog-collar attached to it, so fitted as to give the canine guardian of the position perfect command not only of the flight of steps, but also of the base of the terrace from end to end.

The animal for whose convenience these elaborate arrangements had been made was one of the ugliest and most savage-looking bulldogs I ever saw. He barked furiously, and strained at his chain as if he would tear its links asunder to get at us whenever we looked down upon him from the railings above.

One of our party, a Scotchman, who prided himself not a little on his musical accomplishments, and especially on his proficiency as a performer on the bagpipes, determined to try the soothing effects which a lively air on that instrument would have upon the irritable dog. With this intention he opened the campaign from the terrace. The result was marvellous. The savage brute became dumb at first with terror and amazement, and then uttering his protest against the proceeding in a fit of the most piteous howling, betook himself to the privacy of his kennel, from which no inducement could subsequently dislodge him.

On another occasion, while we were observing the bulldog, a young fox that had been tied up in the yard, broke loose, and came along dragging a piece of rope behind him, which got entangled in a fence post, where he was well within reach of the ferocious bulldog. The latter, seeing the position of affairs, and counting upon an easy victory over such a juvenile and weak antagonist, rushed frantically at the intruder.

Finding escape by flight impossible, the fox made the best of his unfortunate position, and bared his teeth to prepare for the onslaught. The bulldog, however, suddenly changed his mind, and pulled up a couple of yards short of biting distance, where he contented himself by barking angrily, while refusing to come to closer quarters. In the end the fox managed to disentangle himself, and retired without further molestation, leaving the dog's reputation for courage gone for ever. What is still stranger, is that the animal himself seemed quite aware of this, for subsequently, during one of his paroxysms of rage at us, a member of the party, without any weapon in his hand, walked boldly down to confront him, with the result that the dog did not await the interview, but skulked off to his kennel.

Another curious thing at the same hotel was the manner in which the fowl required for table were procured. When they were needed the cook issued forth with an armful of short sticks, about the size of the rungs of a ladder, and so provided, he looked exactly like the proprietor of that popular target known as "Aunt Sally." With serious strides he marched towards the garden, where the rank vegetation afforded excellent cover for fowl during the heat of the day. He was always attended by a boy, to start the game and retrieve the birds that were knocked over, besides collecting the expended missiles for another discharge. According as each frightened chicken was driven across the path, the cook's trained eye took in at once whether it was fit for culinary purposes, and if it was he despatched a wooden weapon after it, that seldom failed to take effect. In this way he generally returned in a very short time, his attendant following him loaded with a full bag of chickens. Occasionally the bulldog I referred to got loose and joined the chase, but he generally came quickly back again, howling loudly, having apparently got in the way of the sticks thrown at the fowl.

The people whose occupation lies at the Paso de los Toros are for the most part a primitive race, engaged in connection with cattle farming and kindred pursuits, together with the tradesmen who supply their wants.

Arising out of these conditions are the industries known as "saladeros," where cattle are slaughtered and their carcasses converted into "jerked beef," for consumption in Brazil and the West Indies. The constant occupation among such scenes hardens men to the sight of bloodshed, so that the taking away of human life is frequently regarded with but little concern, and sometimes even as an act to feel proud of. This is one of the first things that attracts the attention of a stranger upon his arrival in the country. A native talking about a fellow-countryman of his, remarked, "He is a very steady fellow, but not half so good a man as his younger brother. That lad had killed his two men, in fair fight, before he was eighteen years of age."

I had an object-lesson as to the hardening effect produced upon children by being brought up in close proximity to slaughter-houses. As I was walking along one lovely morning, when everything seemed peaceful and quiet, I noticed two boys at no great distance below me. The elder of them was about eight years of age, and the younger one was scarcely four. The larger boy held a little dog in one arm, while with his disengaged hand he sharpened a knife, which, when it had attained a condition to his satisfaction, he drew across the throat of the poor little dog. The blood gushed out, smearing the clothing of the urchins, who laughed with delight over the writhings of their victim. The elder little ruffian could not understand my scolding him for the act, which he considered perfectly justifiable, as he explained to me, in surprise, that the dog was his own.

The drivers of bullock-carts bringing produce and merchandise to and from the railway formed no inconsiderable portion of the floating population.

Vehicles of the kind are not easily guided by beginners at the art, as I know from experience. While riding out one evening I overtook a boy on horseback managing two such carts, each drawn by eight oxen. The owners of the teams were no doubt refreshing themselves at some convenient grog-shop, while they entrusted their carts to the lad to take them to their camping-ground for the night. I readily complied with the youngster's request to take charge of one of the carts while he steered the other through the gateway of a paddock they were about to enter. Irishman-like, I thought the best way to drive was to make the animals stand still until the boy should get the first vehicle through the gate, so that he might come back and take charge of the second one himself.

I had observed his tactics, and followed them closely. Riding up in front of the bullocks I flourished my whip in their faces, and adjured them, as they valued their comfort, to stand still. The stupid oxen, instead of obeying me, made a frantic dash to get past; but I headed them, whereupon, by a rapid flank movement, they completely turned my position, and got away. My instructor roared out his directions to me at the top of his voice, but they proved ineffectual, and he came back to my cart, leaving his own stationary, as he thought. In this he was mistaken, for immediately afterwards we heard a crash, occasioned by the carrying away of the gate-post, against which the leading team had pulled their load in their desire to enter the field

they were bound for. Then followed a volley of
abuse, couched in language so emphatic, that I
understood at once how it was the bullocks had
disregarded my feeble admonition. It was not
what they were accustomed to, or suited to their
comprehension. In their ears it sounded like
childish weakness, which they might disregard
with impunity. It requires an amount of moral
courage, to which I do not lay claim, to remain
silent under undeserved obloquy, and to listen
unmoved to the enumeration of a long list of
supposititious defects of character which, honestly,
I do not think I can be fairly charged with. So
I rode away, leaving the boy still in angry mood.
Upon reflection I decided to be guided by his
advice, and to avoid making a fool of myself again
by attempting to drive bullocks, at all events
until I should have reinforced my command of
Spanish expletives up to the necessary standard.

These same grog-shops (*pulperias*), at one of
which the owners of the bullocks that got me into
trouble were no doubt carousing at the time,
have a very evil influence on the habits of the
people, who are by nature not at all addicted to
strong drink. Houses of the kind are practically

the clubs or meeting-places for neighbours and acquaintances, who are led to treat each other, too frequently with the result that drunken loungers, in a quarrelsome mood, are often to be met with in such places. One frequenter of these resorts, with whom business brought me into contact pretty often, was a festive little magistrate, who greatly enjoyed the company and atmosphere to be met with there. Nor was he always fortunate in his visits to these houses of entertainment. On one occasion he entered a refreshment room where some rough men were drinking, whose ire he managed to excite. Thereupon they carried him out by the legs and arms, and ducked him in a pool of mud. While undergoing the unpleasant process the police came up and rescued the unfortunate man, who was in such a condition that he failed to recognise his deliverers, and drew his knife upon the officer in charge. A struggle ensued, in which he was disarmed, and eventually he spent the night in the "lock up" at the police station.

CHAPTER V

EXAMINING THE COUNTRY

WE began surveying operations at the Paso de los Toros upon the last day of the year 1888, and when they were fairly started I left the rest of the party and went ahead upon a tour of inspection of the route by which it was proposed to take the line.

Our first night out on this separate expedition was one of considerable discomfort. We reached the camping-place after dark, and the only suitable spot that could be found upon which to pitch our tent was very rough and stony. My bed and bedding was left behind by mistake, so that as I had to lie down upon the bare ground, I got but little sleep or rest. But bad as was my plight, I should have been still more uncomfortable had I known at the time, as I did afterwards, that the locality abounded in scorpions and tarantulas. Of fourteen stones that I subsequently turned over by daylight in that vicinity, no less than twelve disclosed the habitation of one kind or of the other of these objectionable acquaintances.

Next morning we made an early start, and although at first somewhat stiff and sore after the night's experiences, I soon forgot all about them. Before I had ridden far we came to a small rectangular yard, surrounded by a low brick wall. The enclosure was what is locally known as a *Campo Santo*, or holy ground, where the remains of the dead are temporarily deposited, awaiting the time when they can be more readily transferred to some graveyard in the vicinity of a town. No attempt at burial appeared to have been made in any case, as coffins in every stage of decay lay exposed upon the surface, while portions of human skeletons were scattered about on all sides. I subsequently saw many other similar temporary receptacles for the dead, some of which, however, were not quite so desolate as the one I have described. A few of them contained rough attempts at what appeared to be provisional vaults. A possible explanation of the apparent neglect to which I have referred might be, that the relatives of those whose remains were lying about may have been killed in some of the numerous revolutions which lay waste the country from time to time, or they may have fled to other lands from some pressing and sufficient cause.

As we went along we met with numbers of ostriches and deer grazing peacefully on the undulating grass lands over which we passed, adding greatly to the picturesque effect of the scene. The ostriches are protected by law, there being a heavy fine for killing one. On the other hand, they are hunted, caught, and plucked of their finer feathers at the season when they are in best plumage, and then set free again to grow another crop for the following year.

For some time after they have undergone this unpleasant treatment they are shy of making casual acquaintances among the human race, and take themselves off into the distant perspective when a man on horseback comes in sight. But gradually, as time wears on, they appear to forget their painful experience about the feathers, and allow one to approach them more closely. Even then there is a limit to their friendliness or indifference, whichever it may be, and when that is past, off go the birds at a trot, pitching themselves from side to side occasionally in a most comical manner, as if mimicking the staggering of drunken men.

It is apparently a game they play, or perhaps the ostrich equivalent for a dance, as each member of the party seems to take it up in turn, and then all of them join in it together, wheeling and doubling, with their wings rapidly thrown out to help the movement, and though perpetually changing places, they never appear to jostle each other.

For the next few days there was nothing of interest to note, until one evening towards nightfall, when we reached a house, from the owner of which I asked permission to encamp upon his land. This he not only granted, but most hospitably insisted upon my dining with him and some friends of his, who happened, he said, to be stopping in his house at the time.

Nothing could be kinder or more courteous than my reception by the entire party, and we spent a very pleasant evening. My host was an agreeable, soft-spoken, mild-looking man, with most affable manners. Next morning he was profuse in expressions of regret that he could not remain to show me more attention, and to point out the best route for the railway in that neighbourhood. But the Government wished for his presence in Montevideo, and had sent up for him, so he was obliged to go; official business could not be put off. I would understand this, he said, and excuse him. Of course I did. I could not be so unreasonable as to do anything else. Later on in the day, when I learned fuller particulars of the cause of his hasty departure, I was confirmed in the opinion that he could not have acted otherwise than he did.

It appeared there had been a double murder in the neighbourhood, and the authorities got it into their heads that my host of the previous night could throw some light upon the circumstance, and had gone through the formality of making him a prisoner, until they heard the explanations he could give of his share in the transaction. That he found the means of satisfying the powers that be was certain, for he was let off and allowed to return to his home. His personal friends made light of the whole affair as far as he was concerned, and blamed the Government greatly for their interference in it. They argued that the two men who had been murdered were ruffians of the deepest dye, and that the doing away with them was a beneficial act, for which the perpetrator of it deserved public gratitude.

It was evident that there were two ways of looking at the matter, though most people might retain a prejudice in favour of due legal formalities being adhered to when capital punishment was in question.

On this same journey, while I was riding at a walking pace over very rough ground, I was approaching a solitary tree growing among rocks, when the man in attendance upon me, who had been loitering behind, unobservant of my movements, suddenly called out to me, in a frightened voice, to stop and wait for him. I did so, and when he came up he caught me by the arm to pull me away from the tree I had got close to, as, if I passed under the shadow of it, it would certainly, he said, be fatal to me. This would seem to indicate the existence in South America of a similar belief to that of the upas-tree.

Other superstitions they have of many kinds. The natives have cures (*remedios* they call them) for every possible complaint of man and beast, some of which are of a curious nature.

There is a skin disease not uncommon in the country, due to severe chills, or sleeping in wet clothes. The eruption follows the course of the nerves, and the people universally believe that if it completely encircles the body, the death of the patient must ensue. This is a belief which I understand prevails in some other countries too; but the cause to which it is attributed, and the cure suggested for it, both struck me as peculiar.

The eruption is said to be produced by the slime of a snake passing over the afflicted person's shirt when spread out on the ground to dry after having been washed. The remedy suggested, which is held by the people generally to be infallible, is to catch a toad and kill it, and then rub the eruption with its dead body.

I was astonished to find a very intelligent and educated Englishman who was a firm believer in the efficacy of this cure.

Perhaps it is the natural antipathy existing between snakes and toads that suggests the idea of the one being the antidote for the other, for undoubtedly snakes are partial to a diet of toads when they get the chance.

Another curious *remedio* was once tried for a horse that I was riding, which had gone lame. The man who was accompanying me told me to dismount, and he would make all right in a moment. I obeyed, as I thought he had detected what had caused the lameness. But instead of proceeding to examine the horse's foot he merely plucked a hair from the fetlock and another from the opposite leg, and placing the hairs in the animal's ear, he muttered something in the nature of a charm or spell, and then told me to re-mount and I should find the lameness gone. I did as I was told to do; but I must confess that I gave way to incredulous laughter, which the operator told me had spoiled the whole effect of the cure. Certainly something had marred its healing influence, for the horse stepped off as lame as before.

Another belief which exists wherever I have been in South America is, that it is particularly dangerous to ride upon a grey horse during a thunderstorm.

One can readily understand that on the plains a man on horseback is a conspicuous object, and may act like a lightning conductor when a thundercloud is rolling along close to the surface of the ground. But why the grey colour should be more attractive to the lightning than any other—bay, for example—I must leave for electricians who have studied the subject to explain.

Proceeding upon our journey, the route we took was by the high land along a spur from the main ridge, and when we came to the end of it the drop down into the valley below was a difficult undertaking, over exceedingly rough ground. Having accomplished it, not without some mishaps, though none of them were of a serious nature, we approached and crossed the river Tacuarembó Chico, and encamped upon its farther bank.

Its course was fringed with beautiful trees, mostly evergreens. In one place the Passion-flower, in rich blossom, had climbed over and almost covered the branches of a thorn-tree. In another there was a beautiful scarlet-flowering creeper, somewhat resembling laburnum in the formation of its blossoms, which had used the support of the widespreading branches of a tall forest tree to display its attractions to advantage.

Our arrival disturbed a number of birds with

showy plumage, and shrieking their complaints at our intrusion, they sought a sanctuary elsewhere.

Another day's march took us to the river Tres Cruces, on the south bank of which we encamped for the night, as darkness had already set in when we reached it.

In the morning we crossed over on a raft made of planks, supported by air-tight barrels, our horses being made to swim. Nor was this latter part of the arrangement so simple to carry out as it sounds to describe it, for they became frightened, and made for the shore among the tangled branches and roots of trees growing by the water's edge. It seemed as if they would get drowned in the wild plunging and confusion that ensued; but the man in charge boldly swam out among them, and with great dexterity managed to get them back into the clear water, from whence they easily made their way to shore.

Soon after crossing the river we passed rough hilly ground, where the soil was barren and the rock showed out on all sides. Away to the east, in the distance, lay the three remarkable hills known as the "Tres Cerros." They are isolated from each other, and rise abruptly from the plain, attaining to a considerable height. Their form in each case is that of a truncated pyramid or cone, surmounted by a vertical castellated wall of natural rock resembling a fortification. This is a peculiarity common to many hills in the north of Uruguay.

Towards evening we reached the river Tacuarembó Grande, which we crossed, and encamped a couple of miles beyond it.

On the following day, when we had risen to the higher ridge, the mining district of Cuñapiru lay spread out before us like a panorama, at a distance of about a league to the right of the course we were travelling; while a couple of leagues farther off in the same direction were the mines of Corrales.

Here our guide became very voluble in describing the untold wealth contained in the district; but do what he could, he was unable to stir up my enthusiasm on the subject to a height corresponding to that of his own, and this puzzled him not a little. The secret was this, but I did not think it necessary to impart it to him: I once had an interest in a gold mine, and my experience thus acquired was not of a nature to occasion me rapturous delight upon visiting a neighbourhood of the kind again. The gold it produced was good and pure, but in quantity insufficient to pay for working. It was then tried for silver, which it also yielded, with a similar result. Copper was next discovered in it, and promised to yield better returns than the more precious metals did.

Here, it was hoped, the downward tendency of our luck might be arrested, but it was not so. When once you have stepped upon the ladder of misfortune and begin to descend it the intervals between the rungs diminish with progressive and wonderful rapidity. The copper, after keeping up for a short time the spurt with which it first led off, gradually followed the example set it by the other ores and ceased to pay. Then plumbago was brought to the surface. It also was good of its kind, but the fatal defect of too great cost of working rendered it practically worthless.

Such was my experience of mining enterprise, and ever since I have looked askance upon possessions of the kind.

After all, that mine was really a wonderful

one. I believe it would have gone on yielding one ore after another until it had got through the list usually treated of in class-books on mineralogy. It would have been most lucrative as a curiosity, if only it could have been exhibited after the manner of a conjurer's inexhaustible bottle. But there was the difficulty. In the nature of things a mine as a whole is not a portable article, that you can take about with you from place to place as if it were a travelling theatre or circus. And to "run" it as a stationary exhibition would have been a hopeless venture in a country where unsuccessful mines with a choice variety of ores are at a discount, in consequence of the supply being far in excess of the demand.

Old reminiscences of this sore subject rose up before me as I looked upon the land of hidden treasure, so that it was not so very strange after all that it failed to excite any great amount of enthusiasm in me.

Towards the end of our journey we reached the vicinity of Rivera, on the frontier. I thought it expedient to encamp some little distance from the town as a precaution against early visitors, of whom I stood in a certain amount of awe, from previous experience of the kind. We arrived at our camping ground too late for comfort, and, as a consequence, had not had a good night of it. Under the circumstances I was not, I fear, in the best of tempers upon being called up shortly after daylight to speak with a gentleman, who announced himself as the "First Official" from the neighbouring town, and wished to see me at once on urgent business. He would not be denied, so I had to get up and hear what he wanted to say to me. I should perhaps explain that the "First Official" is a very important personage, and only second to the *Gefe Politico* himself, who represents the Government, and occupies a position somewhat similar to that of the governor of a province.

The topic of conversation began very wide of the mark of any specially urgent business. My visitor informed me that he was an ardent admirer of, and deeply attached to, England and her people. Then he expatiated upon the merits of his own country and race, in which I could not do less than concur, after his complimentary beginning. Next we wandered off into a discursive chat about railways and their civilising influence upon mankind, while all the time I was longing to get to his urgent business, and to bed again. Seeing that I was conversing with the chief official of the town we were about to enter I suppressed any signs of weariness, and waited patiently for the momentous announcement as to the nature of his special business; but he hesitated to make it.

At last, after a considerable time, he got up to leave, and looking at me with rather a pitying glance I thought, "I observe," he said, "that the señor does not use a razor; but some of his party may do so," adding, "I am a barber, and shall be happy to shave them." Then, as if a bright thought occurred to him, he went on to say, "I cut hair also," glancing at my head as he said so; but the momentary illumination of his countenance faded rapidly away, for I was as closely cropped as a "ticket-of-leave" man upon getting out of gaol.

I shall not trouble the reader with a description of my feelings upon learning the nature of the urgent business for which I had been called up from my sleep at about four o'clock in the morning, after only two or three hours rest; but I fancy the Spartan youth of old, who had to smile and look pleasant while a fox was gnawing away at his vitals all the time, must have felt much as I did upon that occasion.

Before turning in again I thought I should like a cup of coffee, which the cook had very thoughtfully prepared, and while I was drinking it up rode another man, and almost took my breath away, causing me to choke with a mouthful of the hot liquid, too rapidly swallowed, by saying that he was the "first official" of the town hard by.

As soon as I recovered from the choking fit and the shock of this announcement, I stopped our voluble visitor's flow of language by telling him that he must be labouring under some strange hallucination about his position, for there could not be two "first officials" of the town, except they were bracketed equal, like two "senior wranglers," who had got similar marks for their answering. I drew his attention to the fact that we had just received a visit from a gentleman claiming to hold that honourable post, whom he must have met returning on the road.

"Oh! that man," said he, bursting into a fit of uncontrollable laughter, in which I was far too much annoyed to join, "he is only the barber," he pleasantly remarked, seeming to enjoy the whole affair as a capital joke. I was not in the humour to be "done" a second time, so this other claimant for high office was not encouraged to stop. Before going, however, he informed me that he had a well-fenced paddock, in which he would be willing to keep our horses for us at a moderate charge while we remained in the vicinity.

Later on the same morning another horseman appeared in sight coming our way, whereupon I at once retired, expressing my conviction that he was another of the same kind as those who had preceded him. But, even so, I refused to be interviewed again, and lay down to rest.

It may seem incredible, but my prophecy proved to be correct: the new arrival, like those who had put in an earlier appearance, claimed to be a "first official" also. He was vastly amused with the recital of what had taken place, and explained that our second visitor was a messenger of his, whom he sent on errands. This of course I did not hear till afterwards, at second hand, as I was not present at the interview. I forget what particular offer he had to make us; but I may despatch him after the other two with the remark, that neither he nor they had any real claim to the office from which they sought to borrow reflected glory. I subsequently got to know the genuine possessor of the post, and a very different type of man he was.

After inspecting the neighbourhood, we left the town of many "first officials," a description of which I will leave for a later chapter, when we shall have had time to forget the unfavourable first impression conveyed by the redundancy of its officials.

CHAPTER VI

THE HAUNT OF THE OUTLAW

As the surface of the country to be traversed was rough, numerous trial surveys had to be made in order to ascertain the best route to adopt for the railway. One of these took us through a valley, which I have called "the Haunt of the Outlaw," for reasons that shall presently appear, but the name by which it is locally known is the Tambores.

In descending to it from the high land, a rill of trickling water marks the gradual depression in the ground, and it grows by progressive development into a brook, and then a river of importance, bearing along the surface water discharged into it by numerous lateral feeders from a widespread drainage area. Corresponding to the increase in the volume of water are the depth and width to which the valley has been worn out. In the first couple of miles of its course it attains a width of between fifty and one hundred yards, with a depth beginning almost at nothing and reaching to fifty feet, while two or three miles lower down it is some three hundred yards across, and continues widening and deepening as it goes along. At some places vertical rock cliffs, four hundred feet in height, act as its boundaries, and at others it is shut in by rounded or sloping hills.

At one part of the valley I followed a footpath leading up the face of the cliff in order to ascend to the high land, where I hoped to get an extensive view of the country ahead of us. But before I reached the top the path became so steep, that I had to hold on by the mane of the horse I was riding, and lie out upon his neck as far as possible. Even then he stopped short, as if unable to go on, and the man who was following behind called to me to dismount, which I did at once. Nor was the change made one moment too soon, for it was only with great exertion, even when relieved from the extra weight of his rider, that the horse was able to reach the top. Had I remained in the saddle, there was every probability that both he and I might have fallen over the precipice in his struggles to ascend.

Early in its course the water of the stream collects in a deep and placid pool, the surface of which reflects the overhanging crags. This basin acts as a sort of service reservoir, regulating the flow to the river.

On the hill-sides cactus plants of various kinds, with white and yellow flowers, flourish, and the valley below is densely wooded with a growth of timber, chiefly composed of evergreens, the branches of which are matted together by innumerable climbing plants, the whole forming an almost impenetrable mass of tangled vegetation dear to the hearts of outlaws, who can there lie safely concealed from the intrusive eye of inquisitive police. When our surveying party first entered the valley, one of the engineers, standing alone upon an eminence while he sketched the topography of the locality, was surprised to see five or six men on horseback approaching him at a gallop. Not liking the appearance of matters he drew his revolver and called to his comrades, who went to his assistance. They and the attacking party arrived upon the scene at the same moment, and a parley ensued, in which explanations were duly made on both sides. It appeared that the wife of one of the mounted men had gone to the stream the previous day to wash clothes, and that she was captured and carried off by an outlaw hidden in the valley. The bereaved husband had collected some friends to help him in his search for the captive, and seeing the engineer on foot near the spot where the abduction took place, assumed him to be the culprit, a charge of which my friend easily proved himself guiltless. This incident, coupled with some unfavourable rumours I had heard of the Tambores, made me rather suspicious of its character, so when I had to go through it to select the line by which the railway should be taken, I adopted the precaution of having a man to accompany me. As we rode along I made notes of the ground, which, when we had got two or three miles ahead of the party, I wished to send back for their guidance, but did not quite like the idea of being left alone in a place of such bad repute. While considering what was best to be done under the circumstances, I descried a couple of soldiers lying under a tree not far distant from me, and evidently shunning observation. I at once jumped to the conclusion that these were men sent out by the authorities to watch the valley on our account, and keep it clear of objectionable characters; so, taking advantage of the protection their presence afforded, I sent back my attendant to the surveying party with the notes I had made, and lay down in the shade to await his return.

I could scarcely have chosen a more lovely spot to rest in. Near me was a pond, the surface of which was decked with blue water-lilies, while around its margin grew a fringe of evergreens, blossoms of the Passion-flower hanging in frequent clusters from the branches around which the climber had entwined itself.

The moss-covered rocky couch on which I lay was in the deepest shade of a grotto, every nook and cranny of which was clothed with borrowed verdure, maiden-hair and other ferns peeping out from every crevice. In the foreground of the landscape a solitary palm-tree raised its head aloft, while opposite it stood a cactus plant, covered with yellow blossoms, brightening the effect of the picture.

Amid such surroundings I waited in no impatient mood for the return of my messenger, and upon his arrival we proceeded down the valley through other interesting scenes, though not perhaps of equal beauty to that I have described.

Alas! that I should have to confess it, but the truth must come out sooner or later, our railway, when it came to be constructed, passed through the very place where I had rested while waiting for the messenger's return, and grotto, palm-tree, cactus, all are gone, swept away by the ruthless action of the navvy's pick and shovel.

A day or two after our passage through the Tambores Valley the colonel of a regiment lying at San Fructuoso, not far distant from it, hearing where the surveying party was, advised us to be very cautious, as the place, he said, was full of *matreros* (murderers). Upon its being remarked that there could be no great fear of them so long as the authorities sent military patrols through the valley, he seemed puzzled, and asked for an explanation. When told of the soldiers we had seen there he only smiled and replied, "There have been no patrols; the men you saw were probably deserters from my regiment, as twenty of the worst characters in it went off in a body a few nights ago, taking their arms and ammunition with them, and I rather suspected they had gone to the Tambores." This was a new idea for me. Had I known the real character of my supposed protectors at the time when I lay in the grotto enjoying the beauties of Nature spread so lavishly around me, I scarcely think I should have rested as tranquilly as I did.

The fact that the soldiers I saw did not attack me while I was alone and unprotected may have been due to various causes. We were generally assumed to go about well armed, and had the reputation of being good shots. Possibly the departure of the messenger had not been noticed. Besides, although they could only have seen the two of us, they may have supposed that our comrades were close at hand, for I have no doubt they identified us as members of the surveying party. Or they may not have been aware that they were observed in their place of concealment, and thought it just as well not to draw too much attention to their whereabouts.

In order to make matters clearer it becomes necessary that I should anticipate events, and refer now to subsequent incidents that, if traced in strict historical sequence, would give a somewhat disjointed effect to the narrative.

For some time after the construction of the railway works began the presence of our men in the valley did not seem to greatly disturb the outlaws in the woods, who carried on their depredations by night as usual; we were, therefore, obliged to establish a police force of our own, with the sanction of, and appointed by, the Government authorities, to patrol this section of the line. Nor was this measure altogether successful, for we found that the attention of these special police was directed rather to discovering small delinquencies on the part of our own workmen, than to keeping the professional robbers in check. For this reason, after a sufficient period had elapsed to give the working of the plan a fair trial, the arrangement was abandoned. By this time the number of Italians on the works in the locality had greatly increased, and some of them had suffered seriously at the hands of the outlaws, whom they occasionally met on their nightly visits to the drinking shops, which sprang up, mushroom like, on the lands adjoining the railway, notwithstanding all our endeavours to suppress them.

One of these criminals, being very expert with the use of his knife, had at various times stabbed workmen when he caught them alone, so that at last the body generally became enraged at the matter, and determined to take the law into their own hands, with a view to putting down the objectionable custom. For this purpose they met together one Sunday morning in large numbers, well armed with guns and revolvers, and organised a regular *battue*, beating the woods in the valley from end to end. Those sportsmen never boasted much about the bag they made that day, but a couple of dead bodies were found soon afterwards along the route they had taken, suggesting the nature of the game they were in pursuit of. Both of the bodies were recognised as those of notorious murderers, one of whom was the man who had given the Italians special cause of complaint. He was hanging by a rope round the neck attached to the branch of a tree, his body being actually riddled with bullets. That it was a case of suicide was improbable, seeing that if the man shot himself so frequently, in the first instance, he could scarcely have had strength to complete the hanging operation; while, on the other hand, if he began with the latter, he must have had immense vitality, and some one loading for him, and handing him the weapons wherewith to perforate himself in such a wholesale manner. The probability is that the Italian sporting party could have given a more satisfactory explanation of the matter had they felt disposed to do so. One thing is certain, that the neighbourhood was a less popular resort of the outlaws for some time after the occurrence. Many of them fled no doubt from a place that had become too hot to be comfortable or healthy for them, and sought refuge in inferior asylums, just as pheasants take to the hedgerows for a while after the plantations have been shot.

The new locality to which some of them migrated was also upon our line of railway, and a cattle farmer passing through it had a narrow escape from a gang of them.

He had just sold and delivered a herd of fat cattle, and was returning home with the price of them in his pocket, when he rode straight into the middle of a party lying in wait for travellers.

His presence of mind did not desert him; but feigning to think they were policemen in disguise, he remarked, "I suppose you are on some special duty, as I see you are not in uniform?" and then he asked where the officer in charge of the party was.

They replied that he had gone away, but would be back presently, and requested him to dismount and await their chief's return.

"No," said he; "but when your officer comes back, tell him I want him to come up and dine with me," pointing, as he said so, to his house, which was plainly in sight, "and to bring you all with him. I can put the whole party up for the night," he added, "as I am living alone just now. I will hurry on and get ready, and I can go round by the public-house and get something for you to drink as well as eat." So saying, he put spurs to his horse, and rode off without any attempt being made to stop him. No doubt the confederates thought that it would be a still better game to rob the man and his house at their leisure after partaking of his hospitality.

Once out of sight, the farmer made his way to some neighbours' houses, where he got three or four friends to accompany him home to help him to receive his guests. The latter turned up soon after nightfall, and were met by a volley of shots fired at them. They knew at once the trap they had fallen into, and made off.

Next day every hiding-place in the neighbourhood was searched for them, but they had anticipated this movement, and changed their quarters to another district during the night.

I heard several other stories relating to these interesting people, the outlaws; but there was generally such a sameness about the character of their proceedings, that the narration of them would, I fear, prove to be tedious reading. I shall, therefore, restrict myself to a brief reference to a couple of them, that appear to present peculiar features, which remove them from the commonplace category of ordinary events of the kind.

The first of these related to a night attack upon a farmer's house, the proprietor of which was aroused by hearing unusual and stealthy noises about the place. He got out of bed quietly, and after listening attentively, discovered that some people outside were cutting a hole through the door, close to the bolt by which it was kept shut. It did not require any great amount of detective talent to guess the object of the operation, and the best way to foil it was suggested to him by a thong of raw hide with a loop on it that hung from a hook on the inside of the door. Noiselessly removing the thong, he slipped the end of it through the loop, and there he stood, armed with an impromptu lasso, ready for action. A bright moon shone in the sky, diffusing sufficient light within the house to facilitate the preparations for receiving the intending visitors.

It was a very anxious time for the man inside, watching the hole in the door grow larger and larger, until at last it was of sufficient size to effect the purpose for which it was made. There he stood intently observing the opening, as a cat does a mouse-hole, till the supreme moment arrived, and a hand was stealthily inserted not only through the hole, but also through the loop of the little lasso which hung skilfully around it. With a sudden jerk the loop was tightened round the wrist and the hand dragged in as far as the aperture would admit of, while the thong was securely fastened to the hook on the back of the door. In this position the intending robber was perfectly helpless. His companions came to his aid, and having ineffectually dragged at the imprisoned arm till they were tired, gave up the struggle, and prepared to depart.

But they were prudent men, and it occurred to them that to save himself their comrade might betray them. Dead men, they thought, tell no tales, so they cut his throat, and then retired from the scene.

The other incident to which I have referred occurred to a friend of mine. He was riding a young, half-broken horse, when suddenly he observed three mounted men coming towards him in a very suspicious manner. He had incautiously got into a position from which he could not extricate himself without giving an immense advantage to those approaching him, if it became a race for life, in which event he also doubted the staying powers and temper of his untried horse. He had but little time for deliberation, and chose the alternative, to take his stand in a place where his rear was protected by rocks, so that he could only be attacked in front. There he dismounted, and with the horse broadside on, in front, stood behind him, affecting to draw and examine his revolver, for unfortunately he was unarmed at the time. The men galloped down upon him, but as he appeared to be taking steady aim over his saddle, they swerved off to one side or the other when they got within about thirty yards of him. These tactics they repeated several times, their object evidently being to draw his fire on them at a distance where revolver practice would be uncertain, so that they might be able to ride in on him afterwards, before he had time to reload, and finish the matter to their satisfaction. On the other hand, he wished to impress them with the idea that his intention was to reserve his fire until they came to sufficiently close quarters to insure that every shot should be effective. After continuing these manœuvres for some time his assailants held a consultation and then rode away, leaving my friend in possession of the field, from which he too retired immediately upon seeing that the enemy was far enough off to admit of his reaching home without further molestation.

I got a fright myself from falling in with men whom I supposed to belong to the class of out-

THE HAUNT OF THE OUTLAW

laws, but fortunately discovered my mistake in time.

While riding home one evening in company with a young engineer, we passed by a grog-shop, in a lonely spot, keeping at a respectful distance off, as the place had a bad name. A number of noisy men congregated in front of it shouted and signalled to us as we passed by, but we took no notice of them. Two of the party then jumped upon their horses, and galloped down to us in what we took to be a threatening attitude. One pulled aside, but the other came on till he quite got abreast of my companion, so that their horses were almost touching each other. In this position he placed his hand behind his back, under his *poncho*, for the purpose, as I thought, of drawing his knife to stab my friend. I therefore covered him with my revolver, and prepared to pull the trigger the moment I should see the knife appear. To my great relief, however, it was nothing so deadly that he produced, but only a matchbox, as he wanted to light a cigarette.

It turned out that he had been employed upon our surveys, though we did not recognise him at first, and his intentions were altogether hospitable, not hostile. He wanted us to have a drink with him at the public-house close by, where to all appearance he had already imbibed too much himself. We thanked him, but declined the kindly meant offer, and proceeded homewards, while he went back to the attractions of the grog-shop.

To return to the valley of the Tambores. Even after the professional outlaws were expelled from its precincts, all was not quite so peaceful in that happy region as one could have desired. The workmen occasionally had their own little differences between themselves, which were settled in the usual way, by the arbitration of the knife. The results appear in the grass-covered graves, surmounted by wooden crosses, that are to be seen, all too frequently, along the line of railway, and in one instance that I recall, in a triple row.

The railway company have established a station in the Tambores, which they call by the rather fanciful name of the "Valley of Eden." The only connecting link between the place and the name that I can think of is the presence of the serpent, which is well represented in the Tambores. Perhaps I am a little sore upon this subject, as the railway authorities rejected with a touch of scorn a suggestion of mine, that they should give their station the appropriate title of "The Robber's Rest."

CHAPTER VII

WATCHMEN

WATCHMAN, what of the night? is a reasonable question to ask if one is anxious for information on the subject; but there is this drawback to the value of the knowledge thus acquired, that its accuracy is frequently open to considerable doubt. It is a pity that such should be the case, but it is to be feared that uncertainty of the kind will continue to prevail until the guardians of the night adopt more careful means to make the news which they proclaim aloud agree approximately with actual facts than has hitherto been the custom with them. It tends to shake one's confidence in the correctness and precision of a force, the members of which frequently disagree about such a plain and uncontroversial matter as the hour of the night.

For example, take such a case as occasionally occurs. A watchman arriving round the corner of a street publicly announces in a sing-song voice, intended to be musical, that it is just two o'clock, when another, whose slumbers he has probably disturbed, takes up the information incorrectly, and proclaims the hour as twelve, both the numbers sounding somewhat alike in Spanish.

A citizen whom their noise awakens strikes a match in order to look at his watch, and see which of the two is right, and finds that both are very far astray, the true time being say half-past four o'clock. Is it likely, when that person turns over in his bed for another sleep, that his mind will be in the peaceful condition conducive to repose? I fear not. He is far more likely to let his angry passions rise, while he calls down all sorts of imprecations upon the heads of the erring officials, whose blundering has marred his rest.

But these observations are only of a speculative nature, and I do not think that the people of El Paso de los Toros had given their minds to any contemplation of the kind when first the subject of these remarks came into prominence among them, whatever may have been their opinion about it later on.

The place had a character which people unfriendly to the district professed to think might easily have been better. In fact, life there was not, upon the whole, so quiet and monotonous as one might expect from the isolated position of the town.

Some of the inhabitants were of a lively and enterprising disposition, and kept up a certain amount of excitement by sundry acts, that those in authority viewed with disfavour.

A curious circumstance connected with the case was the frequency with which the accidental discharge of firearms took place, and, stranger still, it was not in single shots at a time that this usually occurred. When the weapon was a revolver, there was generally a series of five or six discharges on such occasions, according to the number of chambers it had. If its owner was asked to account for the circumstance, he invariably was quite unable to do so. That the revolver went off of its own accord, without any provocation from him, was all he could say about it. Generally the bystanders were more frightened than hurt on these occasions, but the result was not always equally innocuous. In one instance the bullet went through an inoffensive spectator and lodged in an equally innocent passer-by, while in other cases wounds of a more or less dangerous nature were inflicted. There were several houses in the place, the walls of which bore bullet marks, both inside and outside, giving evidence of their having "stood fire." Querulous people there were who suggested that where events of the kind were so numerous they could not possibly have been all accidental, and there appears to be some force in this view of the case. But, for my own part, I have had so many narrow escapes myself from the accidental discharge of firearms, and I have known other persons with similar experiences to mine, that I am not disposed to press doubts of the kind too far, or to be too dogmatic on the question of design or accident in such matters.

There was a very deplorable and tragic occurrence at El Paso de los Toros while we were there. A most respectable and steady young man, while fiddling with a rifle, which he did not know was loaded, shot his mother and his sister, to both of whom he was deeply attached. The one died immediately, and the other in a few hours after the accident. But this is a digression indulged in for the purpose of showing that some of the discharges of firearms that disturbed the public nerves may have been purely accidental. That there were others the design of which did not admit of any doubt, is but too certain.

Nor was the chance of being shot the only danger of which the peaceful inhabitants complained. The knife was a weapon that did its work silently, and far too frequently to be agreeable.

In this condition of affairs the public mind became alive to the necessity of adopting measures to stop unnecessary killing, and attempts at it, and even robbery; or, at all events, to reduce these occupations to more moderate figures in the crime statistics of the district. The outcome of all the deliberations on the subject was a general agreement that the best plan to accomplish the desired reform was to supplement the exertions of the ordinary preservers of the peace by establishing a strong and efficient body of night watchmen, under the control of the police authorities.

This decision was hailed with public approbation, and law-abiding people willingly subscribed towards the cost of carrying it into effect, in the hope of reducing crime to a minimum.

The matter was undertaken with becoming spirit and determination, and no time was lost in completing the necessary arrangements. Men congratulated each other when they met, and "stood treat" on the strength of the happy era about to be inaugurated.

At last the eventful day arrived, the night of which was to usher in the new order of affairs. Men of unblemished character, sleepless vigilance, and innumerable other good qualities had been selected to form the force of watchmen. They were duly paraded, reviewed, and addressed, amid the acclamations of the populace, who were greatly pleased to hear that the safety of their persons and properties were to be entrusted to such a band of heroes. There was not a man in that force that did not leave the parade-ground with the highest opinion of his own merits, and the assured belief that he had done more for the salvation of his country—a form of expression that is very popular, and does not seem to mean much—than if his personal valour and strong right arm had gained many decisive victories for her.

When the proper hour came round the watchmen went on duty. "*Nox erat; et bifores intrabat luna fenestras*"; and the reason "the moon entered at the windows with their double shutters" was because people took no trouble to close their shutters that night. Why should they, when their houses were protected by such vigilance and valour?

In the discharge of his duty upon that occasion one of the new guardians of the peace was proclaiming to the inhabitants, whose entire confidence he possessed, the hour of the night, the state of the weather, and that everything was everywhere tranquil, when his statement was rudely cut short, and his unfinished assertion contradicted, by a loud report in his immediate neighbourhood. It was the usual thing—a revolver shot, and the man who fired it was arrested, but could not account for the trick the mischievous weapon had played him. He had only taken it out of his pocket to make sure that he had it on his person, when it went off of its own accord in the most absurd way.

The circumstance was passed over without much comment, and matters settled down quietly into daily, or rather nightly routine.

Like children with a new toy, we were greatly interested in the watchmen at first, but before long we got tired of listening to their monotonous information.

For my own part, I confess that I was guilty of an attempt to corrupt those members of the force who were stationed in our immediate neighbourhood to the extent of requesting them to give as little public information as possible during the small hours of the night; or, if the conscientious discharge of their duty in this respect was not to be tampered with, that they would make their public statement from time to time regarding the hour, the weather, and the peaceful condition of the town in a colloquial tone of voice, instead of resorting to the high-pitched key that awoke the soundest sleepers.

I hope I shall not be considered by purists in such matters to have been guilty of any gross bribery in arranging to supply the two watchmen whose "beat" was nearest to us with a cup of hot coffee each night at eleven o'clock. The result I found conducive to my own sleep and, a cynical friend added, to that of the watchmen also.

After a time people began to complain that there was no perceptible reduction in the amount of nightly crime that was committed, and public attention was directed to the matter by two or three exceptionally bad cases which occurred just then. There were the amateur detectives too—young men addicted to keeping late hours—who boldly asserted that the watchmen slept peacefully in quiet nooks and corners all through the night.

These charges caused the chief of police to investigate the matter for himself, in order to see if they had any foundation in fact. With this intention he went the rounds unexpectedly one dark night and found the public guardians slumbering peacefully at their respective posts. He therefore captured and removed their lanterns, but did not disturb the sleepers.

Next morning, at the hour for the watchmen to give in the night's report, the different ways in which the loss of the lanterns was accounted for would lead one to suppose that an extraordinary epidemic, with varied symptoms, had broken out among those useful articles. When the watchmen's powers of invention were exhausted they were shown into a room, in which the missing lanterns stood all arranged in proper order; nor was their pleasure at discovering their lost property half so great as might have been expected. That episode was a deathblow to the force. It gradually faded and withered, and before long ceased to disturb the nightly slumber of the citizens.

For our own purposes we had, however, to employ night-watchmen to look after a large quantity of railway sleepers and other materials liable to be stolen or to be set on fire. Nor were we always successful in securing the most suitable men for the service.

One New Year's morning the chief of police called upon me at an early hour, and after we had exchanged the friendly greetings of the season, he drew a revolver from his pocket and handed it to me, saying it was mine. I replied No; that my revolver was in my bedroom. "I don't mean the one you carry yourself," he said, "but that it belongs to your company," and then he went on to explain that during the previous night his sergeant had been twice fired at, and the second time they caught the culprit, and found him to be our night-watchman, who had some outstanding grievance against the sergeant. The chief disarmed the man, and had a sound flogging administered to him. He then gave him back his knife, but retained the revolver, telling him to continue on duty as watchman for us, and that if he did not find him at his post the next time he went the rounds, he should get another taste of the lash.

I thanked the officer for his thoughtful consideration of our interests, and of course dismissed from our service one who was so anxious to distinguish himself in the rôle of murderer, as our watchman appeared to be.

Another night our two watchmen had a difference between themselves, which they fought out for their own amusement, one of them overcoming and disarming his adversary. He generously abstained, however, from following up the usual rule of *væ victis!* In fact, neither suffered much, only receiving a few scratches, but they lost their situations.

While sitting up late one night a shot was fired close to my door; when I went out to see what was the matter I heard the sound of the retreating footsteps of some one running away, and then followed the report of two more shots. I waited for a while to listen if anything particular was going on, but as I heard no further noise, I set the matter down to the fault of somebody's revolver going off of its own accord as usual.

Another night I was aroused from my sleep by four or five shots fired in quick succession quite close at hand. There seemed to be a general engagement going on in the yard behind the house. I seized my revolver, a weapon which, in that country, is always kept, like the candle and matchbox, within easy reach, in case of being needed in a hurry, and opened the back door, where I found our watchman standing outside in a very excited state.

His account of the matter was that he had come upon a man in the act of getting in through my bedroom window, and had promptly fired at him, not once only, but four or five times, and although he was quite satisfied some of the shots had taken effect, the intending burglar had managed to make good his escape in the darkness of the night.

CHAPTER VIII

POLICE

THERE exists in the minds of some persons a strong antipathy to police, as a body, both at home and abroad. Perhaps the feeling may be due to unreasoning prejudice, or partake of the nature of the constitutional objection which burglars are understood to entertain to the presence of bulldogs about a house, the interior of which they desire to inspect.

For my own part, like most people who have travelled a good deal, and penetrated into strange places, I have made acquaintance with the police of many lands, and not always in the most friendly way. Indeed, there have been occasions when I considered myself badly treated by them. Still, on the whole, I have no great fault to find with police, as an institution, and until the world at large becomes a trifle better behaved than it has hitherto been, it is somewhat premature to expect, or even hope for, the dissolution of the recognised guardians of the public peace.

In Uruguay I was not, I fear, always in the best of tempers with every member of the "force," as, for example, when I met a policeman, as I did more than once, mounted upon a horse of mine, that he had ridden almost to death, besides giving him a sore back, that rendered the animal useless for weeks together. The ready excuse on such occasions was, that his own horse had broken down, and meeting with a stray animal on the way, which turned out to be mine, he had pressed him into the service, as he was bound to do. That was the official version. The real one was that, having been sent on a long journey, the policeman went to our paddock, where he knew the horses were well-fed and in good condition, and took a temporary loan of one of ours, without going through the formality of asking permission. After a while, however, we managed to get a stop put to this class of annoyance.

Most of the police officers with whom we were brought into almost daily contact, in consequence of the large number of labourers employed upon the railway works, were pleasant and satisfactory to deal with, and of some of them I must speak in the highest terms, in consequence of the excellent manner in which they discharged their duties. In many cases of emergency too, they rendered me most energetic and effective assistance.

There were other persons in authority also, to whom I was frequently indebted for timely and important information, that enabled me to frustrate designs which had been made against us.

Our headquarters, as previously mentioned, were at first at Paso de los Toros, which has been already described. Our office consisted of a corrugated iron hut, including rooms for myself and a servant, and we were obliged to be very watchful on the nights when large sums of money had to be kept in the safe to meet the requirements of the monthly pay-days.

On several such occasions I received information that different gangs of robbers were ambitious to relieve us from the responsibility of keeping the cash which caused so much anxiety. I did not enter into particulars about such matters with my servant, though he was entirely trustworthy, as I wished to keep them as private as possible. I merely warned him to be very careful about keeping the doors and windows shut at night when we had much money in the house, no matter how hot the weather might be at the time, and also to be particularly on his guard not to get into conversation with strangers, or to mention anything about our habits or affairs to outsiders. One evening, after nightfall, upon returning to the stables to leave my horse there, I received private information that a strong gang of well-known robbers had left Montevideo and come up country with a view, it was thought, of visiting us that night, as it was one of those occasions on which we had to be careful. While pondering on this serious news I came suddenly round the corner of the office, and found my servant deep in conversation at the yard gate with some one whom I did not know. I took a sharp look at him, however, before he moved away, and when he had gone I asked my man who he was. "Some stranger," was the reply. "What was he saying to you?" I continued. "He only wanted to know who lived in the house, and what rooms we slept in," he made answer. I thought this incident, following so closely upon the warning I had received, was very suspicious, so sought at once an interview with the chief of police, to whom I told all I had heard, giving him at the same time as good a description as I could of the stranger I had seen at the gate. "I'll go," he said, "and see if I can make anything out of it, and let you know the result." In the meanwhile I got my dinner, and inspected our arms and ammunition, to see that all was in order, and ready to hand in case of being required.

About an hour afterwards the chief of police returned and reported that all was right, as he put it. "I have found the men," he said; "they are a pretty strong gang, too, and the man you saw at the gate is one of them. They have engaged rooms for the night at the inn opposite, and are playing billiards there now. I am going over to have a talk with them, and I shall see you later on." With this he went off, but returned towards midnight, when the information he had to give me took somewhat this shape. Upon leaving me, earlier in the evening he had posted men on the look-out near each of the public-houses in the town, to watch for the gang in case of their changing their quarters, and to report their movements to him. This done, he went back to the billiard-room where he had already seen them, and finding matters going on as before, he managed to get into conversation with the strangers, asking many questions. While so engaged an acquaintance of his came in, and addressed him by the title of his office, whereupon he saw a look of intelligence pass between the men he was watching. Presently they left the room, and soon afterwards word was brought him that they had gone to another inn, where he also went, and discovered they had taken lodgings for the night there too. He then visited the billiard-room, and expressed surprise at meeting them again; but they soon moved on elsewhere, and he followed them, questioning them closely about their movements. This time they resented his pursuing them in so marked a manner. In reply, he explained it was part of the duty of the police, of which body he had charge, to observe the movements of all strangers, and to prevent their getting into any unpleasantness or trouble, especially when notice of their coming had been announced by telegram.

He then told them openly that the authorities

had sent warning to be on the watch for them, that their plans had been made known, and a particularly warm reception was prepared for them. His men, he explained, had been watching them all the evening, and would not lose sight of them that night, no matter where they went, if they remained in the neighbourhood.

This settled the matter; they saw their game was up, and they quietly left the town, passing over the railway bridge, which was the only way, except by the ferry-boat, of returning again. At both places he left a couple of policemen on guard with rifles, and then came to tell me of the steps he had taken, as I have narrated them. "I thought it better," he said, "not to wait for a shooting-match in the night-time, when all sorts of accidents and mischances might happen, and perhaps the wrong people get shot. You can go to bed now," he added, "and sleep comfortably, for they will not come back again when they know that we were advised of their movements beforehand."

He was right about their not returning, though I was not able to follow his advice altogether.

Sleep won't always come exactly when one

wishes for it; besides, I felt I had better keep in a state of preparedness during the night, and postpone my sleep till after daylight. I never told my servant what a near thing it was that night, nor the character of the man he had been talking to at the gate, and I feel sure he thought I had allowed myself to be absurdly concerned about trifles on that occasion.

This incident, taken in connection with one mentioned in the preceding chapter, where our night-watchman fired at a man trying to get in through my bedroom window, and the private warnings I so frequently received, besides meeting with suspicious persons lurking about the place at night on different occasions, made me very watchful during that anxious time. But my position would have been much worse had it not been for the efficient assistance so readily given me by the chief of police.

Another night burglars made an attempt to break into one of our huts at the Paso de los Toros, but were discovered in time, and their scheme frustrated. I think they must have belonged to a different gang of robbers, and probably mistook the house they attacked for the cash office.

We had other causes of anxiety also, by reason of the fact that the money for our monthly payments had to be brought up from Montevideo by a night train, as the day train did not suit bank hours.

Our accountant conveyed it, always travelling with a companion, both well armed. Then there was the further process of transmitting it up country to pay the various sub-contractors, which had at first to be done by an armed party travelling on horseback. According as the rails were laid use of course was made of them for this purpose, and a monthly pay train, well armed, was sent over the line.

While this system was in full working order an intimation was once given me by the proprietor of a public-house in a lonely neighbourhood to be specially careful, as he felt sure an attack upon the pay train was contemplated. His suspicions were aroused by the conduct of a man from a very bad locality, who had been spending a couple of days at his house without any visible business. Our informant observed that this stranger made many inquiries about the means we adopted for sending the money over the line to pay the workmen, asking all sorts of particulars about our pay train and its movements. Nor was it only from the public-house people that this information was sought. Whenever any workmen from the railway came in the stranger plied them with similar questions. Thus forewarned, we took extra precautions. The pay train was well manned and armed, and drove very carefully past all suspicious places. No attack was made upon it; but I was not the less obliged to the friendly publican who had given us warning; for I thought it by no means improbable that some plot of the kind had been in contemplation, though it was not carried out.

On one occasion a determined and elaborate attempt was made to wreck a train of ours under circumstances that looked as if the object was robbery. The police authorities felt sure that such was the intention, and that the people who made the attempt mistook the special train, for which the plot was laid, for a pay train.

A tour of inspection of the works, by some officials, had been arranged, to begin about fifty miles up the line, and to extend onwards from that point. As there was a long day's work before us, it was decided to start a couple of hours before daylight, so as to begin inspecting as soon as we could see to do so. We had also to avoid getting in the way of the material train, which went out to the front every morning with rails and sleepers. It was therefore settled that it should follow, and pass our "special" at the place where we were to begin operations. These arrangements were duly notified up the line the previous day, so that everything should be off the rails, and the way clear for our special an hour earlier than the usual time for the passage of the material train.

Some delay occurred in starting, so we had to alter our plan and let the material train precede ours. We followed it in due course, and when we arrived at the station where we were to begin inspecting, we found the material train waiting upon the siding there, getting some repairs done to the engine. It appeared that shortly before daylight it struck against a pile of sleepers which had been placed upon the rails, and packed carefully into an open culvert. The material train was a very heavy one, and running at a high speed at the time, there being a stiff gradient to surmount just in front of it, so that it knocked the obstruction off the rails, but kept to them itself. Had our light "special" been the one to meet with it, the result might have been very different.

CHAPTER IX

PERILS BY LAND AND WATER

In the course of our proceedings we met with, or witnessed, many adventures, the recital of some of which may not be uninteresting. The first of these that I will mention occurred in the following manner :—

The Chairman and the Managing Director of the Central Uruguay Railway having come out from England to the River Plate, it was arranged that they should drive through the district to be traversed by our line, so as to obtain a better and more intimate knowledge of the country with which we were dealing. Several other gentlemen connected with the undertaking joined the party, and I accompanied them.

Our means of conveyance consisted of a heavy, lumbering coach, called a *diligencia*, drawn by ten horses. The chairman and I sat in an open seat in front, as he wished to get a good view of the country through which we were to pass, while the other gentlemen occupied the interior of the vehicle. In this way we started upon our journey, and soon found that our horses, which seemed so unnecessarily numerous at first, were not too many, as the roads were heavy, and we had some difficulty in getting over the bad places. Towards nightfall we came to a spot where there was a depth of about three feet of thick mud. The horses entered it willingly enough, and did their best to take the vehicle through it, but the wheels only sank deeper and deeper in the mire. After they had struggled in this way for some time the iron pin connecting the body of the coach with the front axle broke off short, and away went horses, pole, axle, and driver, whose hands were entangled in the reins, all together, while we were turned over into the mud.

I got a kick on the head in the fall, which stunned me for the moment, but a man of mine, who was travelling with us, rescued me, and brought me to more solid ground. As soon as I recovered sufficiently he took me to a pool of water and washed the dirt off me, just as if I had been a horse that floundered into it.

The chairman got off very safely, nor were the inside passengers much the worse for the upset. The driver was an energetic man, and soon had the breakage repaired, and was ready to go on again, so that the results of the disaster were not very serious after all.

The remainder of our drive that day was not far, and we stopped for the night at a small wayside inn, of very limited accommodation. It had but one room for strangers, into which we put the chairman and the managing director; another member of the party slept on the kitchen-table, while the rest of us took shelter in an outhouse. There we snatched such sleep as we could during the intervals of peace conceded to us by a most aggressive family of cats, that looked upon our arrival on the scene as an unjustifiable invasion of their territory.

I may here observe that the upsetting or breaking down of public conveyances is by no means an unusual experience in Uruguay. Several people connected with the railway met with accidents of the kind from time to time, and our material trains frequently rescued belated travellers who were victims of mishaps of the kind.

Nor was it only from the overturning of vehicles that inconvenience arose. There were other accidents of various kinds perpetually happening. Four times in one day did horses fall under me. Two of these incidents were trivial affairs, but the other two were rather serious. I will only refer more particularly to one of them, the results of which were painful enough for a time. I was riding back to our encampment one night after dark, when my horse stumbled over something, and fell with a crash. In trying to get upon his legs again he threw back his head, which struck me full in the face with the force of a sledge-hammer. One of my assistants, who was riding with me, sprang to the ground and helped me to get down, and supported me until I was sufficiently recovered to stand alone. As soon as I was able I remounted and rode on to our tent. When we arrived there my nose was found to be broken, and almost flattened to my face, and one of my fingers was much crushed.

The latter was soon bandaged, and then I directed my attention to the injured nose, which I worked into as good a shape as I could, and bound it up, with the aid of my friend, who was as handy and attentive as a trained nurse would have been, and did everything in his power to relieve my suffering.

In the morning I was in the saddle and at work again soon after daybreak, with my face so closely wrapped up, that there was nothing visible of it but the eyes. Gradually my wounds healed, and I was able to discard the protection for my nose, of which a doctor friend of mine told me I had made a very fair job. It is true that at the same time he took somewhat from my pride about the surgical skill I had displayed in the matter, as well as from my personal vanity, by asking me the suggestive question, "Was your nose always crooked?" I tried to lessen the sting implied in his remark by persuading myself that it was due to professional jealousy.

I will now turn to that part of the subject which relates to perils by water. The Latin poet tells us that the rustic waits for the river to flow past. He evidently thought that the rustic was an example of imbecility, for he adds, "but it flows on, and will continue to flow, through every revolving age." Our own late poet-laureate probably had these lines in his mind when he made the brook to say, "but I go on for ever."

It is quite clear that both authorities were thinking only of streams, the habits of which were regular and above reproach, and not of such as display their force and progress with intermittent energy, changing from dried-up watercourses to foaming torrents, and *vice versâ*, within the space of a few short hours.

Had Horace or Tennyson visited the River Plate, and travelled much in the interior of that country, he would, no doubt, have discovered from his own experience that the rustic was not such a fool as many people might suppose him to have been.

In rainy weather, waiting for the river to flow past is one of the commonest occupations of daily life in Uruguay. A man rides up to a ford, and finding it too deep and rapid, after recent rains, to attempt to cross with safety, quietly dismounts, unsaddles his horse, and ties him to some tree or peg. He then sits down to smoke a cigarette, and at nightfall rolls himself up in his poncho, and turns over to sleep upon the leather bed provided by the trappings of his cumbrous saddle, patiently awaiting the morning's light and the hoped-for subsidence of the river. What else can he do in a country where there are no bridges except those upon the railways?

I have known a little stream that I have repeatedly jumped across on foot spread out to a width of more than a hundred yards, with a depth of from ten to fifteen feet, in five or six hours, and fall again as rapidly.

Nor was it the smaller rivulets and brooks alone that changed their character so completely according to the rain that fell. The larger rivers, too, felt the influences of alterations in the weather equally, though not, perhaps, with quite so great rapidity.

One of these, the Tacuarembó Chico, is a good example of the kind. In its normal state everything suggested peace and tranquillity; but I have also looked upon its waters in a very different mood.

Rain had fallen in torrents, and a destructive flood arose, converting the usually placid stream into an angry rushing torrent thirty feet deep, and in some places half a mile in width.

As I gazed in wonder on the scene, a solitary

boat with two men in it came drifting along among the tree-tops, where the current was least. They seemed looking for something which the flood had carried away, and in reply to my inquiries told me that the object of their search was the son of one of them. The hapless child had strayed into the woods to gather wild flowers, and his return was cut off by the sudden rising of the water. The body of the victim was never found, but lay no doubt amidst the general desolation, as did also the carcasses of numerous cattle that had been similarly surrounded, and unable to find their way back to dry land.

While residing at the Paso de los Toros I saw a most impressive, I might almost call it a terrible, flood in the Rio Negro. During one rainy season it overflowed its banks, but at first no one thought much about it, or expected it to rise to any dangerous height. As time wore on matters looked more serious. The poorer huts along the margin were the first invaded, and one after another had to be abandoned. The more solidly built houses, that stood on higher ground, were reached in due succession, while hour by hour the water stole up the side walls, silently but surely blocking first the entrance doors, then the windows, and lastly submerging the roof of each luckless building. Those who lived in them fled towards higher land, some in boats, others on rafts hurriedly extemporised from the doors of their deserted houses, and cowered in a wet and miserable plight till the flood, after rising to a height of sixty feet and more, began to subside again. But bad as was this inundation, it was not so formidable as one that occurred in the same locality not many years before.

I did not witness this previous visitation, but I saw photographs of it, and heard descriptive particulars of its rise and fall from several persons whose business required them to examine closely at the time into the question of its magnitude and the effects produced by it. It rose much higher than that which I have already described, and reached to about three feet above the surface of the rails upon the Rio Negro bridge, the under side of the superstructure of which is more than sixty feet above the ordinary height of water in the river.

All traffic upon the line was impossible, and I was assured by the general manager and by the resident engineer, that large snakes and curious wild animals, which had been carried down upon floating trees from Brazil, were found resting upon the girders of the bridge.

This inundation completely destroyed a great portion of the old town, and huts had to be erected on a high promontory to accommodate the houseless sufferers.

Nor was my knowledge of such terrible floods derived solely from beholding them as a spectator standing on dry land, at a safe distance from the destructive scene enacted by the rushing waters, or from hearing the graphic descriptions of them from those who had witnessed their effects.

I had myself personal experience of the horrors of immersion in the maelstrom of a torrent of the kind, and of the exciting struggle against its relentless fury.

I came one day to a river that was swollen till the water flowed through the tops of the trees growing upon its banks. Thinking that, perhaps, Horace was right after all, and that the river might go on flowing deeply, if not for ever, at all events for a sufficient period to be very inconvenient for me to remain like the rustic, waiting for it to flow past. I determined if possible to get over at once. The only way to cross it was by means of a frail temporary raft, upon which I embarked under the guidance of an Italian sailor, with the result that it sank beneath the two of us in mid-stream, and left us floundering in the torrent. Fortunately I succeeded in grasping a wire that was stretched between the banks, and with its aid I pulled myself along until I got to calm water, and found a submerged branch of a tree upon which to rest my feet. The pilot, who was an expert swimmer, and not overweighted with heavy clothes as I was, recovered the raft, and towed it into the "back-water," from which he reached me with ease, and brought me to the land. A young engineer upon the bank awaiting his turn to be ferried over threw off his coat and boots when the accident occurred, and prepared to plunge into the water to come to my assistance. It was with difficulty, too, that he could be persuaded to desist from the attempt, although it would have been utterly useless to try to swim across a current of such velocity.

On another occasion I was travelling in a wagonette drawn by three horses harnessed abreast, when we came to the ford of a river that looked rather swollen. Every care was taken to examine it, and the general opinion was that we might safely drive across it. It was, however, desirable to lighten the load as much as possible, so we descended from the vehicle and rode over on horseback, leaving the driver alone to guide it across.

Matters proceeded satisfactorily till he had reached the middle of the stream, where some confusion took place, and the horses became restive and began to plunge wildly, when all at once they moved a little to one side and got out of their depths. The wheels of the wagonette had become entangled in the branches of a fallen tree lying in the bed of the river, and could not be moved one way or the other. The pole-straps kept the horses' heads down, so that they made furious struggles to try to free themselves.

Three men that accompanied me did everything in their power to release the struggling animals, but it was no easy task to perform.

At last it was accomplished, but not till more than an hour had been spent in the endeavour. One of the horses was so much exhausted that he had to be towed to the river bank, where his head was supported, and he was left to recover strength, but he succumbed and died in a few minutes. A second horse had strength enough remaining to swim to shore; while the third, known by the name of "the Tiger," from his vicious disposition, when freed from the trammels of the harness, turned round, and, instead of swimming for the shore, clambered into the wagonette he had previously helped to draw; nor could he be dislodged from his position as an inside passenger until he had rested for some time and regained a portion of his strength. Both the surviving horses had suffered so much, that it was some months before either of them was sufficiently recovered to do ordinary work again.

The crossing of flooded streams was a perpetual source of trouble and accident to us. Many a time has a horse fallen under me while fording a river, and sent me head foremost into the water. I don't suppose there was an engineer connected with the work who did not frequently experience the sensation of taking an involuntary bath of the kind. But it was not always a fit subject for mirth or amusement, as twice during the progress of the works such accidents had fatal endings.

CHAPTER X

LANDOWNERS, WORKMEN, ETC.

AFTER the difficulties which the want of regular roads and bridges occasioned us, I think I might place the obstacles arising from our dealings with landowners. In saying so, I am bound in fairness to admit that many of them showed great favour to the railway, some even giving their land for it gratuitously, while others aided us in different ways.

It is, however, with the majority, not with the exceptions, that I am now dealing.

One curious phase of the matter was the immense amount of local information voluntarily supplied to us by the people living in the districts through which we passed when making the preliminary surveys. It was often of a most contradictory nature, necessitating much care and trouble to sift it so as to separate the grain from the chaff.

If we could credit them, it would almost appear as if the inhabitants of Uruguay were born with a natural aptitude for selecting lines of railway. They always knew, or at least said they did, the best possible route to follow, irrespective of its length or such minor considerations as curves and gradients, viaducts or tunnels.

After a varied experience of their ways I have come to the conclusion that they are as full of expedients for diverting railway surveyors from their own lands to those of their neighbours, or *vice versâ*, according to what they consider to be most conducive to their private interests, as a hen-lapwing is in her endeavours to lure away unwelcome intruders from the vicinity of her nest. Like her, too, they occasionally become very angry if their little stratagems are unsuccessful, and swoop down upon one with denunciations almost as shrill as hers.

Some of them content themselves with uttering dark threats of vengeance on the part of the powers that be, who, by a strange coincidence, always seemed to be nearly related to, or on terms of great intimacy with, these slighted landowners.

Others, of a more fiery nature, place greater

trust in their own right hands than in official partizanship, and publicly proclaim their preference for bloodshed, with a determination to resort to it upon the first favourable opportunity that presents itself.

There was wonderful unanimity in the nature of the advice given to us by all persons of the former class with whom we had dealings, though it frequently bore very different meanings.

Each one of them was confident that we were giving ourselves unnecessary trouble in making any further surveys, or in searching for any other line for the railway than that which he recommended. Besides, we were told we might rest assured that it would certainly be the only one sanctioned by the Government.

This was perplexing, for the lines suggested possessed varieties of position and direction that were perfectly irreconcilable.

Conspicuous among the fiercer landowners was one with whom our relations were anything but friendly at first. He hated the railway and railway people.

One wet and stormy night I reached his house, and finding that I could not get any farther, and that there was no other place for miles around where I could get shelter, I asked for it from him, but was unceremoniously refused. I was told that I might sleep outside in an open shed if I chose. This was a most unusual piece of discourtesy in South America, where the people pride themselves, and justly so, on their universal hospitality.

The owner was kind enough to give me warning that if he ever saw me upon his land anywhere away from the line of railway, he would "shoot at sight." As he bore the reputation of being as good, or as bad, as his word, I did not spend much of my time trespassing upon his property. I had to ride across it frequently, however, and once I had to pull down part of his fence to get a bullock-cart through it; but on such occasions I kept a good look-out for the enemy, and was always careful to see that there were no empty cartridge cases in my revolver.

The wheel of fortune in its revolutions brought about a state of affairs when it was in my power to do this man a material service, and I did it. At first he could scarcely believe the fact, but when he grasped its reality, he became one of my warmest supporters, and remained so till the end.

As a mark of special friendship — I may mention the fact, though it is anticipating events—when I was leaving the River Plate he was anxious to bestow upon me a lively collection of wild animals, in which specimens of the carnivora were well represented.

The intention was kind, but I could not see my way to accept the proffered gift; it is so difficult to arrange satisfactorily and comfortably for the establishment of a menagerie about a country house in Ireland. If you keep the beasts locked up they will howl and roar at night, making sleep precarious, if not impossible, for wakeful people. Or if you try the alternative plan, and let them loose, the neighbours, especially those who keep cattle, sheep, or even children, might not like it; and it is always unpleasant to be on unfriendly terms with one's neighbours. For these reasons I had to disappoint my generous friend, and deny myself the pleasure of possessing an interesting collection of the kind.

There was another landowner very similar in many respects to the one I have just described. He also hated the railway and all belonging to it, and was equally explicit as to his intention to shoot any of us he caught trespassing upon his property.

On one occasion, while on a tour of inspection, I was stopped by a flooded river, and found that I must either cross the land in question or make a deviation of several miles. In this dilemma I rode straight to the owner's house, explained the matter to him, and asked his permission to continue my journey over his property, which he gave me without any hesitation.

Nor are railway engineers the only people who get mixed up unpleasantly with land questions in Uruguay. Surveyors engaged in defining the limits between properties frequently meet with difficulties in the discharge of their duties.

One St. Patrick's Day I received a telegram from the authorities asking me to send an engine with some trucks to one of the stations on the railway, to bring back wounded men and prisoners. The request sounded quite natural and home-like, and I concluded that some enthusiastic people had been celebrating the day a little too well, and had got into trouble. But my conjecture was altogether wrong. No Irishman was mixed up in the quarrel; nor had St. Patrick's Day anything to do with it, except the accidental circumstance that the fighting took place on the eve of that festival.

I heard all about it afterwards from some of the persons who took part in the affray.

It arose in this way. A party of surveyors was employed to mark out the boundary line between two properties, and as they proceeded, the man who employed them, and at whose house they were stopping, was well satisfied with the manner in which they were performing their work. Not so, however, his neighbour, who thought that some of his land was being taken from him, and he determined to make a struggle to maintain his rights. His plan of action was prompt, but not of a nature to recommend its general adoption in questions of disputed boundaries. He decided to make a night attack, with the aid of his friends, upon the surveying party, and for this purpose entered into negotiations with one of the latter's workmen to betray his employers, and open the door of the house for the attacking party. They would thus be able to surprise the inmates in their beds, and make short work of them. Everything was arranged, and when the conspirators reached the yard gate, in the night time, their confederate duly opened it and admitted them to the enclosure. There he left them while he stealthily entered the house by one of the windows, so that he might open the door for them. He did so without delay, and the next moment they were received with a volley fired from within the house. The workman had told his employers of the plot against them, and the assistance of a party of police had been obtained to repel the attack. A general fight ensued, in which one man was killed on each side and several wounded; in the end the aggressors being beaten, and many of them made prisoners. It was for the purpose of bringing in them and the wounded that we were asked to send out a train.

The question of disputed boundaries often gave us much trouble, but I have said enough to show how serious it may become at times.

As I already explained, all the landowners

were not unfriendly to us; but besides those I have mentioned, there was a third or intermediate class, who for a long time remained very reserved and distrustful in their dealings with us. In several cases much trouble had been taken to prejudice them against us.

One man in particular comes back to my memory, to whom we had been painted in anything but pleasing colours. Great exertions were made to induce him to take legal proceedings against the railway company for imaginary injuries of various sorts, but he withstood all the alluring offers that he received in respect of assistance in matters of the kind. For some time after I made his acquaintance he evidently looked upon me with great suspicion, and was very cautious and reserved in his dealings with me. Gradually, however, I gained his confidence, and the reserve was changed to feelings of mutual respect and friendship, which continued unbroken till we said good-bye and parted at the close of the works.

Here I must say something of the workmen by whose labour and toil the railway was constructed. The great majority of those that we employed were Italians, who came principally from the northern and mountainous districts of their native country. As a rule, they were hard-working, cheerful, well conducted, and not difficult to manage. A reference to them in the chapter upon the " Haunt of the Outlaw " shows, however, that at times they could take the law into their own hands, though it should be remembered that in the case referred to they had received great provocation.

Like other rough men, they had their quarrels, and did occasionally resort to the evil practice of using their knives to settle such disputes; but even so, and when actually engaged in fighting, they were comparatively easy to control. As an example of this, I may quote an instance that came under my personal observation.

Upon one occasion, as I turned an abrupt corner, I found myself among an excited crowd of spectators, looking on at two Italians fighting fiercely with their knives. The combatants at once obeyed my order to stop and give me their weapons, apologising for their conduct as they handed them to me. I scarcely think that two of my own countrymen could have been so easily separated if engaged in a serious encounter of the kind.

We had a good many Austrians and Bavarians from the Tyrol, who were mostly masons or quarrymen, and particularly satisfactory and pleasant to deal with.

There were but few Spaniards upon the works, and they were chiefly Basques, a hard-working, strong, and thrifty race.

Of the workmen who were natives of Uruguay I ought to have a kindly word to say, as they mostly served me well. They are not adepts with the pick and shovel, but they are very intelligent and handy men, and at their own particular occupation of looking after horses or horned cattle they have few equals.

Of course I do not mean to say that all our workmen were perfect, and that they never gave us trouble. On the contrary, there were some of them whom I should have to describe quite differently if I went into particulars. We had the usual strikes and threats to deal with, but, thanks to the energy of the *Gefe Politico* of the district and the assistance he gave us, we got fairly well out of our troubles of that description.

One great difficulty we had to contend against during the progress of the works was a serious outbreak of smallpox.

It began at the Paso de los Toros, and soon developed into a very formidable epidemic. The police bestirred themselves well to meet the emergency, and erected a wooden hospital, for which we helped to provide the materials.

When I went to look at the result of their labours, I was somewhat shocked to see that they had placed the building exactly opposite the gate of the public cemetery. I remonstrated with them about this, and said it would have a very depressing effect upon the inmates of the hospital, to which the police sergeant, who was in charge of the party, replied, " But then, señor, it is so very convenient for the burials." I remember a precisely similar arrangement of hospital and cemetery in the case of a continental town, that always seemed to me to have been a most unwise selection.

The Government sent up a medical inspector to report upon the outbreak. When he came to the Paso de los Toros he found the temperature in the hospital there too high, and ordered the windows and doors to be all opened wide. The weather was piercingly cold at the time, and it was said, with what truth I know not, that six deaths followed immediately upon the sudden change of temperature. It was further stated that two of the patients, who had witnessed this result, were so frightened, that they took the first opportunity to get out of their beds and made their escape, nor were they heard of afterwards.

The epidemic spread rapidly, extending to San Fructuoso and Rivera, which places it visited with considerable severity. Nor was this surprising, for the general inhabitants took little precaution against it; and as vaccination did not appear to have been in common practice, people lacking that protection, when they came in the way of contagion, ran all the greater risk of catching the disease.

I have seen a beautiful little girl, of about twelve years of age, carrying in her arms a baby in the worst stage of smallpox, and as it was highly improbable that she had been vaccinated, one could not but shudder at the thought of the danger she was incurring.

But if the public generally did not do much

to counteract the ravages of the disease, societies of charitable ladies were formed in the various centres of population, who did their best to fight against it, and to relieve the accompanying distress.

CHAPTER XI

LITERA SCRIPTA MANET

THE headline of this chapter is one of those general assertions which are nearly as often wrong as right, and yet I have some hesitation in attacking it, for it is a maxim dear to the members of the legal professions, among which bodies I have many valued friends. It seems to yield them a somewhat similar consolation to that which, we are told, the sonorous word *Mesopotamia* afforded the good old lady when learned discourses became too abstruse for her simple understanding.

It is the one spot on the lawyer's chart where he thinks he may anchor with safety during the fogs of uncertainty or squally weather, so prevalent in legal navigation; but outsiders like myself may be pardoned for entertaining some doubt about the matter, notwithstanding that the information is conveyed in a dead language to give it greater force.

At one period of my life I looked upon the truth of the maxim as unassailable, and on a par with the arithmetical dogma that "two and two make four"; but the experience of years has weakened rather than strengthened my confidence in this respect.

It is useless to tell me now, either in English or Latin, that "the written letter remains," when I know to my cost that it sometimes flies away, like a bird, on the wings of the wind.

In support of my present incredulity I will mention a few cases, from many, that are decided exceptions to the asserted rule.

The weather was exceedingly hot, the thermometer marking over 100° Fahrenheit in the shade, as I sat down one morning in my hut at El Paso de los Toros to read the letters that had just come in from the post-office. The windows in the room were wide open, and not a breath of air was stirring. The first operation was to sort the correspondence, and distinguish between what apparently related to the works and that which was private, "business first and pleasure afterwards." I had exhausted the first category, and opened a fat-looking letter of the second, that seemed to promise an abundant yield of information. It began well, and I turned over to read the name of my correspondent, as I did not recognise the handwriting.

Just then a noise behind me attracted my attention, and I looked to see what caused it. A "whirlwind" was passing by, and occasioned the rustling sound I had heard. Having ascertained this, I turned back again to go on with the reading of my letter, but observed to my surprise and dismay that it was passing through the open window and circling upwards out of reach. I rushed after it hastily, and sent one of our men in pursuit of the flying letter, telling him to watch carefully where it might fall, and bring it back to me.

After the lapse of a considerable time the messenger returned, looking hot and crestfallen, for he was obliged to confess that he had been unsuccessful.

"Señor," said he, "I followed that letter of yours all the way to the Rio Negro, and I do believe it contained the prayers of some good person, for there it was wafted up to heaven out of my sight." After such an experience, is it not mockery to tell me that "the written letter remains"?

I wonder if the reader can sympathise with me in my disappointment at the loss I sustained. One as a rule gets so few nice letters, and this was a charming one, as far as I had glanced at it. It is so disappointing to think that I never knew who wrote it, and that it has remained unanswered to this day. I only hope the writer of it may read these pages, and see in them the explanation of my long silence and apparent rudeness. I appeal to every person who ever wrote me a letter to which no reply was returned to recognise in that lost document the one so left unanswered, and to accept this public explanation and apology for my compulsory share in the transaction.

I met with another case where several written letters did not remain. We were crossing a river, in which there lay floating about what looked like a number of envelopes. Upon closer inspection they proved to be unopened letters, which we collected, dried, and then forwarded to the post; and it is to be hoped they eventually reached their respective destinations.

The mischance in this case was probably due to the upsetting of a *diligencia* in the river, no uncommon experience, and the falling out of some of the correspondence from an open letter-bag into the water. Perhaps it may be argued that this example rather goes to support the legal view of the case, because the written letters did remain in the river till we fished them out of it. My contention, however, is that they did not remain in the mail-bag, which was their proper place till sorted for delivery in the post-office in the regular way.

Another case where the written letters did not remain occurred to a friend of mine at the Paso de los Toros. He had arrived by train, and after placing his portmanteau and a bag containing a voluminous correspondence in his bedroom on the ground floor, threw open the windows and went out to enjoy a cigarette under the shade of the veranda. While so occupied he observed a man, bag in hand, coming out of his room; but this did not surprise him, as he thought it was some one who was retreating upon finding that he had opened the wrong door by mistake. The man, as he passed by, made some polite apology for mistaking the room, and my friend thought no more of the matter till some time afterwards, when, wishing to look at his letters, he went for his bag and found it had been stolen. Here, surely, the written letters did not remain.

A somewhat similar trick was tried upon me, but not in the same place. I had a despatch-box full of business documents and correspondence with me in a tramway-carriage, and when I reached the terminus I got out, leaving it behind me on the seat while I helped some lady passengers to descend. Having done so I went for my despatch-box, but it was nowhere to be seen. At that moment I observed a man with what looked like my missing property hurrying away rapidly, and I followed at once in pursuit. When I overtook him I claimed the box he was carrying off as mine, but he boldly asserted it was his own. I explained that my name was engraved upon a brass plate on the lid of my box, and insisted upon the cover being unstrapped, to prove to whom the property rightfully belonged. When this was done the justice of my claim was apparent, and the man, with profuse apologies for what he called his stupid mistake, returned towards the tramway-office to search for his own despatch-box. On his way to it he suddenly disappeared round the corner of a street in the most unaccountable manner, and, strange to say, no article of the kind was claimed or found by the tramway people on that occasion.

In this instance, again, the written letters did not remain, though it is true they were recovered and brought back.

Perhaps objection to my views may be raised on the ground that the maxim in question only applies to legal or public documents, and not to general correspondence. Even so, I am prepared to show that in that sense too it is frequently falsified.

Proceedings in the Landed Estates Court have shown that the title-deeds of numerous properties in Ireland have been lost, and cannot be recovered.

I know of an instance, too, where the sale of a branch railway to a main line cannot be, or, at all events, is not, perfected because the title-deeds for the land it occupies are not forthcoming.

Nor is it in Ireland alone that documents of the kind go astray. I had personal knowledge of a number of valuable title-deeds having been rescued from the ignominious fate of being sold to a retail grocer as waste-paper in which to wrap up his wares. And this occurred in London, where one would expect them to be guarded with especial care.

Once when searching through the manuscript records of an important public body I came upon a blank of several years, caused by the cutting out of the pages relating to them.

Who has not heard of erasures in baptismal registries when they disclose inconvenient facts? One constantly meets with passages similarly treated when examining old manuscripts. Gravestones have even been known to be mutilated to prevent the legend on them being produced as evidence in legal proceedings. Sometimes cases of the kind arise from carelessness or vandalism. I possess a photograph showing an example of the latter. It is of a grave-stone, on which are carved the arms of a very ancient family long since extinct and forgotten in the district except by antiquaries, while under the arms is boldly cut into the stone an inscription of only a few years ago, in memory of a man of the labouring or small farmer class, of a totally different name and family to that to which the arms belonged, and evidently without any intention of establishing any connection between them. It would appear that the stone in question was a fallen one which belonged to an unknown grave, and that it was dug up in the process of preparing the ground for a new burial. As the inscription on it was almost obliterated, it was thought to be of no value, except as a headstone for the new grave, for which it came in handy. It seems a great pity that some one should not have interfered to prevent the act; but probably it was not discovered till too late.

I know of no class of document but one that seems to have any claim to such permanence as suggested by the maxim I am dealing with. It is that which comprises the department of correspondence commonly described by the term, "love-letters."

Their tenacity of existence is beyond dispute when one reflects upon the certainty with which they are forthcoming, in profusion, in all cases of breach of promise of marriage tried in court, to the utter discomfiture of the faithless swain, and the enjoyment of a virtuous public, that rejoices in the triumph of right over wrong.

After all, I may perhaps be told that the meaning of the maxim is not that which I have given to it, but that it is simply equivalent to saying it is safer to put the terms or conditions of an agreement in writing, than to trust to the retentiveness of the memory to reproduce them when necessary. If so, why not have said as much in language that did not admit of any doubt?

CHAPTER XII

SAN FRUCTUOSO

SAN FRUCTUOSO, or Tacuarembó, as it is also called, is the only intermediate town upon the extension of the railway with which we were engaged. It is situated 110 miles from the starting-point, or about 280 miles north of Montevideo, and some 72 miles from the Brazilian frontier. It has a population of about 3000, and lies in the valley of the Tacuarembó Chico, on the right bank of that river, upon low land, the soil of which is a sandy loam.

The town is approached from the south by a road, along the sides of which grow aloe hedges, that appear to be impenetrable, by reason of the formidable spikes with which Nature supplies that plant as a protection against all foes. The aloe is the porcupine of the vegetable kingdom.

These hedges extend for some distance within

the limits of the town, till they give place to wire fences with timber posts, and these again to walls of brick, less picturesque, but more suitable and convenient for enclosing human habitations.

The houses are all one storey high, and most of them have flat roofs, although a shed or sloping roof is occasionally to be seen. The dwellings of the poorer classes have a very bare and unfinished look, but possibly those that attracted my attention on this account may only recently have been developed from the primitive mud *ranchos* of the original settlers.

Some houses, on the other hand, exhibit every sign of comfort and prosperity, being surrounded by gardens and enclosures full of flowers, shrubs, and climbing plants, Wistaria being conspicuous among the latter.

In one place I saw a tall hedge of roses, with a small pink flower about the size of the Banksia kind; in another, a fence composed of quince-trees, with their delicately-tinted blossoms like those of an apple-tree.

The principal public square is planted with Eucalyptus and other Australian trees, which seem to flourish well in Uruguay.

The inhabitants of the town congregate in this square on fine summer evenings to listen to the music of a military band, while breathing the cooler air that comes with the approach of night, and is rendered all the more enjoyable after the scorching heat of the mid-day sun.

A peculiarity about the promenading upon these occasions is that ladies and gentlemen keep strictly apart, and one seldom sees them intermingle.

Another source of amusement, though of an intermittent kind, which the people of San Fructuoso possess, consists of a small but well-appointed theatre, where sometimes travelling actors make their appearance.

San Fructuoso, like other towns of its kind, was not without its fair share of enterprising, though unpleasant inhabitants. I refer to the class the members of which prefer to make other people support them, to working honestly themselves. Their calling was usually followed by night, and in the unfrequented suburbs.

One of our men was attacked in a lonely spot, but managed in the struggle that ensued to disarm his antagonist, and carried off a huge knife, which he took from him, as a trophy of victory. On another occasion an attempt was made to rob and murder an Italian, who was on his way to his duty at night as cleaner of an engine. He, too, was expert with his knife, and gave his assailant some ugly gashes, only receiving scratches himself. The aggressor finding that he was getting the worst of the encounter blew a whistle, and immediately a couple of policemen came running up from a house close by. The robber with great presence of mind gave our man in charge for an attempt to murder him. He had managed to get clear of his knife, and the only weapon to be found was that in our man's hand, so that he was arrested, and before he could get out had to pay a fine of fourteen dollars for a murderous and unprovoked attack upon a peaceful citizen who was going about his business. At least that was the view the authorities took of the case.

Another time a member of the staff, walking along the road on the outskirts of the town after dark, saw a man suddenly appear before him going in the same direction. When he reached a lonely spot the man in front stopped and turned round. My friend immediately stepped out into the middle of the road to proceed by it, such being a very usual precaution to take in that country. The man on the pathway also walked out and barred his passage. Upon being remonstrated with he replied that the road was a public one, to the use of which all people were equally entitled. "Good!" said my friend, "you shall have your choice; take either the main road or the pathway, whichever you wish, and I will go by the other; but if you attempt to stop me, or approach me, I will shoot you without further notice," and suiting his action to the word he covered the man with his revolver. After a moment for reflection his opponent gave way and allowed him to pass on unmolested, only muttering some disparaging allusions as he did so.

There is nothing in San Fructuoso calling for special notice, but some of its surroundings have considerable interest for those to whom Nature in all her varied phases presents never-ending attractions.

Upon the river Tacuarembó Chico, which flows past it, one gets many glimpses of tranquil beauty from a boat floating down the current in its normal summer condition. The width of the stream then averages from forty to fifty yards, with a depth of nine or ten feet, though in places it is only two or three feet deep, affording good crossing for those on horseback.

Here and there a double channel surrounds an island, where wild fowl live a life of retirement for the most part undisturbed. Then, again, the surface of the water spreads out in a picturesque bay, along the margin of which aquatic plants, with flowers of various colours, form an indeterminate boundary. Both banks of the river are for the most part thickly wooded. Willows with a delicate yet luxuriant foliage, unknown in colder climates, dip the points of their weeping branches into the stream as it ripples past. Forest trees make their appearance here and there, while evergreens in endless variety, among them a very fragrant one of the myrtle family in full blossom, occupy the intervening space. The crimson-flowering Mimosa, with its brush-like blossoms, is to be seen on all sides; nor are climbing plants unrepresented in the general display. Bright yellow and delicate mauve-coloured bignonias hang from the branches of the trees around which they have entwined themselves, contributing their full share to the brilliancy of the scene. When the sun is not too high the light and shade cast upon the varied foliage intensifies the general effect; but, if the heated glare wearies the beholder's eye, a soothing change is easily obtainable by looking at the mimic representation of the scene mirrored in water as smooth as glass.

Animal life adds interest to these surroundings. An occasional water-hog (*carpincho*) plunges into the river from the bank on which he lay basking lazily in the sun, uttering a bark-like grunt as he disappears. The giant kingfisher drops from some overhanging bough upon his finny prey, or betakes himself to a more distant post, protesting, with discordant chatter, against the disturbance of his retreat. Two lesser relatives of his there are that occasionally follow his example and contribute to swell the volume of complaint.

While rowing in these placid waters one often sees the dwarf-heron, the smallest of its tribe, standing scarcely six inches high. It is a beautiful little bird, with slate-coloured body and yellow legs, a black crest and dark beak, also dark covering feathers to the wings, and a brown stripe down the breast. White herons and others of ordinary slate colour, exactly like our own at home, from time to time fly up from some sequestered nook as we row along, and seek retirement elsewhere. In the thicket the calandria sings to his mate upon her nest, while from the glades beyond the fringe of trees the plaintive whistle of the larger partridge (*martinetta*) gives warning of the approaching close of day. As we turn a sudden bend in the river's course, a flock of doves with a couple of hawks, frightened into strange companionship by the approach of a common enemy, fly off and leave us to pursue our course till darkness falls upon us, and the night-herons come out to follow their calling in company with the vampire bats.

Near where I lived there was a placid lake, on which the willows growing on its margin were so clearly represented, that it was difficult to say where the tree itself ended and its reflected image in the water began. Gay-coloured blossoms of various aquatic plants decked the surface of this lake in summer, their leaves matted together forming floating islands, upon and among which a numerous young family of water-hens were wont to disport themselves.

They were most gaudy birds of the kind, possessing red bodies and golden-coloured wings. Such is a correct description of them when flying, but when on the ground or in the water, they appeared to be altogether red. It must, therefore, have been the under side of the wings only that was yellow.

Here, too, might frequently be seen a pair of white herons standing patiently upon the bank, awaiting a fitting opportunity when some foolish young frog or other edible delicacy ventured within reach of their long, sharp bills, to show with what unerring swiftness and dexterity they can strike their prey.

Any description of San Fructuoso and its surroundings that did not embrace some notice of the "fern grotto," not far distant from it, would give but an imperfect impression of the locality. Thither I will now ask my readers to accompany me, and to rest for a while beneath its grateful shade, while I endeavour to reproduce, though in dim perspective, some of its leading features. It lies hidden away among the hills, and one comes upon it unexpectedly, if unaccompanied by a guide. It is a perfect little gem of almost tropical scenery, wholly unlike the character of the surrounding country. It would look as if it had been transferred from its natural position by some magic power to a more southern latitude, where men might view its beauties under more comfortable conditions than are attainable in the torrid zone.

The name, however, is somewhat misleading, as there is no cave or grotto to be seen, but only a glen flanked by steep rocky cliffs of most picturesque appearance. Through it runs a rippling brook, the banks of which are clothed with a rich growth of ferns in great variety, among them being two flowering kinds I had not seen before. Large trees, with branches covered with mosses and orchids, afford both shade and shelter to tree-ferns varying in height from fifteen to nineteen feet. The fronds of these latter are of immense size, and delicately formed, shooting from a stem almost worthy of a palm-tree, and hanging down in graceful drooping curves. Here and there beautiful flowers interpose between the ferns, upon those favoured spots where sunlight falls with unimpeded brightness, making up patches of colouring that would charm an artist's eye.

The whole effect is lovely and soothing, and it makes an impression upon the memory that is very pleasant to recall. The power of Nature is displayed in a manner so lavish, that were one to try to copy it on canvas, the fault of overcrowding could scarcely be avoided; yet looking around on all sides, I defy the most critical observer to suggest a single alteration that would improve the general effect.

You would, perhaps, remove that fallen tree or those withered fern fronds, and leave nothing but what was fresh and young and beautiful to be seen? My friend! you would paint your landscape without lights and shades upon it. It should present no hint of death or of decay. A pleasant composition truly! but only suited to hang upon the walls of Paradise, and not well calculated to appeal to beings such as we are, with the force of Nature's own treatment of the subject.

CHAPTER XIII

IN THE GARDEN

THERE are few places where a busy man can spend a more enjoyable half-hour, when he happens to have the rare good luck to be able to indulge in an extravagance of the kind, than in his garden. When so engaged his surroundings exert a soothing influence on his mind, and tend to smooth the asperities only too often incident to the occupations of an active life.

There is much to learn from observation on occasions of the kind, if one enters the enclosure with a mind prepared to receive instruction from the best of all teachers, Nature herself, and to carefully preserve the impressions thus derived in the storehouse of his memory.

I hope it was in some such spirit as this that I strolled into the garden one bright sunny day, repeating to myself, while I walked along—

"As the sunflower turns on her god when he sets,
The same look which she turn'd when he rose,"

for a number of these golden blossoms attracted my attention. But my poetical quotation was cut short before I got more than half through the verse, for the flowers themselves, of which the poet sang, were flatly contradicting his statement regarding their habits. There was the sun high up in the sky, and not one of his floral worshippers had turned to look at him. On the contrary, they were mostly looking at each other, or on the ground; but none of them ventured to stare up straight overhead, perhaps from the fear of getting a sun-stroke.

Surely the poets (for many, both ancient and modern, have written on the subject) cannot have meant that the regard of the sunflower for the luminary of the day was of an intermittent nature, restricted to a look turned towards him twice in the twenty-four hours, when he rose in the morning and set at night. Moore, at least, cannot have intended to convey an impression of this kind, for the lines which follow those I have quoted clearly indicate that the gaze of the sunflower towards her god was of a continuous nature, following his diurnal track in the heavens. One can't help feeling just a little sorry for the sunflower, and unwilling to mention anything that would tend to lower its status. This is especially the case when we reflect that not so long ago it was brought before us by the professors of æsthetic art as being the most lovely and high-class flower of the garden, "a thing of beauty and a joy for ever." It was to form the model by which those people who set up for culture should regulate their lives.

Alas that it should be so! but it is sadly to be feared that these professors were themselves blind leaders of the blind, for as the sunflower faded, the lily blossomed forth in all its purity, and a new æsthetic prophet told us to worship and live up to it.

Philosophers of this cult are lavish in their praises of its superiority to anything of the kind that had hitherto appeared. This may be so, but, for my part, I should not consider the life it necessitated as altogether one of self-denial.

As to the purity of the lily, that is indisputable, and it furnishes a high example in this respect; but the plant possesses other characteristics that may not be generally considered so worthy of imitation. For example, it leads a proverbially sluggish and idle life, and has an amazing power of absorbing liquids, qualities to which man is sufficiently prone, especially in hot climates, without the necessity for any extra encouragement to cultivate such habits.

Perhaps these little difficulties might be overcome by substituting as the exemplar a less thirsty flower for that popular favourite, the lily of the Nile.

Close beside the sunflowers in the garden stood one that I could recommend, a white trumpet-lily. It is true that its petals had a delicate, crimson-coloured, feathery marking which took somewhat from the purity of their whiteness; but then the flower was abstemious enough in the matter of drinking to satisfy the most rigid teetotaler, though I can't say whether it is less lazy than its Egyptian relative.

There is a gorgeous flower of the same family, somewhat like our Scarborough lily, but I suppose that would shock æsthetic tastes; and, after all, to live up to a scarlet flower is more than can be reasonably expected from ordinary mortals.

Leaving worshippers of the higher art to settle all such questions relating to the objects of their adoration, we, with humbler pretensions, may occupy our leisure moments in a survey of the pleasant scene before us. Beautiful flowers grow luxuriantly on all sides, so that the eye rests with satiated pleasure on its surroundings.

Nor is it inanimate Nature alone that supplies objects of interest to the observer. While gazing at the flowers I almost trod unawares upon an army of black ants that were endeavouring to force a passage through the territory of their red relations. The latter are of much smaller size, but they make up for any deficiency in this respect by an extra venomous and fiery disposition. It is wonderful how quickly one of them can dispose of an antagonist so much larger than himself, as the black ant is. His usual plan of action is to begin by biting off his foe's legs, and when he has finished this part of the operation he quietly hoists the mutilated trunk on to his back, and walks away with his load, to hide it in a place of safety as an article of food for future use, just as a dog secretes a bone when he is not hungry, or has not sufficient time to devote to the consideration of it at the moment.

With the red ants it is not easy to get on friendly terms, they are so prone to treat all overtures of the kind with distrust, and to meet them with hostile demonstrations. With the black ones it is less difficult to arrive at a *modus videndi*, especially out of doors. As an engineer I am naturally interested in all industrial proceedings, and bound to watch with pleasure the work of these busiest of creatures. But when it comes to the building of ant-hills, about the size of small haycocks, on one's bedroom floor, the annoyance and inconvenience far outweigh other considerations, and it becomes necessary to protest against a trespass of the kind.

The worst of it is, that they look upon all such remonstrances as unreasonable, and this produces strained relations, which frequently end in open war. My experience is, that if once you begin to fight with ants, whatever may be their colour, there is no peace to be had till every one of them is driven out of the locality or otherwise accounted for.

There were other inhabitants of the place, or rather migratory visitors to it, that spent much of their time in the garden. They were the humming-birds, the most charming little creatures in existence. As they darted about from flower to flower, with the sunshine reflected from their feathers, they looked as if they were animated gems — emeralds and rubies. At times when they rested, perched upon a telegraph wire, and twittered their experiences to each other, one could almost fancy they were part of a fairy creation.

Very friendly feathered acquaintances in the garden were the oven-birds. They seek the dwellings of men, and build their nests in their vicinity, apparently for safety and companionship. The bird is not quite so large as a thrush, of a brown colour, and has an unmusical song of its own, of which it is quite as proud in its way as the nightingale might be of its unmatched performance. The name is derived from the character of the bird's nest, which is a round, dome-shaped structure, built of mud, and bearing some resemblance to the primitive baking ovens one occasionally meets with in the country. It is divided internally by a partition into two compartments communicating with each other,

L

that next the door doing duty for an entrance hall, and the one inside being the dwelling-room, or nest proper.

At first I thought the two rooms suggested a rather conceited sort of bird, that fancied itself higher in the social scale than most others of the feathered tribe, which are content with one apartment. The nest being roofed in I did not mind so much, for many other birds also adopt that wise arrangement. A peculiar strut in the oven-bird's walk seemed to corroborate the idea as to its having an exaggerated opinion of its own importance.

In this estimate of its character I was wrong, and I now publicly retract it, and apologise for having attributed such unworthy motives as pride or conceit to the oven-bird.

I had an opportunity of seeing the great practical advantage of its style of domestic architecture. A pair of birds of this description built their nest on the cornice of the house in which I lived, and their young family were brought up in it, and almost fledged and ready for flight, when a stranger called to visit them one day while their parents were absent. It was by no means the sort of acquaintance that the old birds would have chosen for their children, for the visitor was no other than a kestrel. It alighted at the nest, the door of which was too small to admit of its entering, but it stretched in first one of its claws and then the other, and made several attempts to seize and drag out some of the young inmates. At this point I came to their rescue, and the kestrel flew to a tree close by, where it watched my movements, coming back to the nest when I went away, and renewing its attempts to get at the young birds, but unsuccessfully. Had there been only one room in that home, it is scarcely probable that the attack of the hawk would have ended fruitlessly as it did.

There was a further interest for me attaching to this particular nest, for when the oven-birds were done with it, and their young ones had grown up and gone out into the world, two swallows took possession of the nest, attracted to it, possibly, by the recommendation of its burglar-proof qualities, and brought up their family in it also.

I may here mention that the swallow proper of South America is not the same bird as the

European one, being larger and clumsier, and having a less sharply forked tail than the latter. But as regards house-martins, after repeated and close observations of them, they seemed to me to be the same in both countries.

It was not only in the daytime that the garden proved an agreeable retreat. Frequently in the evenings I used to sit there, breathing the cool refreshing air after a day of more than usual heat in summer, and gazing at the Southern Cross, which I would have willingly exchanged for the Ursa Major of the northern hemisphere.

It must be confessed, however, that the voices of the night, breaking the surrounding stillness from time to time, were sometimes neither musical nor attractive. There is an extraordinary race of frogs inhabiting the neighbourhood of a lake close by the garden I have been describing, that "mew" like a cat. Their vocal performances are evidently controlled by a single conductor or bandmaster. In the midst of the most profound silence, one may be startled to hear what seems at first to be the mewing of a cat. The spell is broken, and a thousand other throats take up the cry, repeating it with monotonous iteration, until at some preconcerted signal all stop together as suddenly as they began. Then the large frog of discontented mind and grumbling habits, never tired of airing his own grievances in a note of deepest bass, addresses the assembled multitude, receiving croaks of approbation from time to time when he makes a point of more than usual force. I feel certain that the subject of his discourse, whenever I have listened to him, was always the same—a strong denunciation of the railway people, who had drained his native swamp to some extent, thus lessening his "marshy joys." In fact, his estimate of the progress of his country was that it was going from bad to worse with the speed of an express train and the ease with which the Latin poet tells us the descent to Avernus can be made, a sentiment in which the others of his kind appeared to concur unanimously.

Next came the little green tree-frog, that addressed the audience in a musical voice, with a metallic ring in it. This family take a much less depressing view of things in general than that entertained by the preceding orator. They sing in chorus a more lively refrain, that seems to indicate a belief in the approach of better times.

Lastly, there was a frog in that neighbourhood with a voice like the note of a policeman's whistle, which he often sounded when he thought that the others had been discoursing or occupying public attention too long. This frog seems to discharge a somewhat similar function among batrachians to that for which the *clepsydra*, or water-clock, was used by the ancient Greeks—to regulate the period allotted to speakers.

As regards its peculiar note, several times have I been startled by it, thinking that a policeman was calling for assistance.

But by far the most weird of the voices of the night was the cry of the brown stork. The first time I heard it I was going into the garden, when dreadful shrieks, that seemed to be uttered by some one in great agony, reached my ear. I felt sure a murder was being committed quite close to me, so, revolver in hand, I rushed to the spot from whence the sounds seemed to come, but could find nothing to account for them. I feared that I had come upon the scene too late to be of any use, that the crime had been already accomplished, and the victim's voice silenced in death, while darkness favoured the murderer's escape.

In pursuing my search I disturbed a stork of the kind to which I have alluded, and it flew away, repeating as it went off a series of dreadful shrieks similar to those that had at first startled me, thus affording an explanation of the mystery of the moment.

CHAPTER XIV

THE FOUR-LEAFED SHAMROCK

"I'll seek a four-leafed shamrock" sang the minstrel, and, if I remember rightly, in the event of his search being successful he expected to become surpassingly fortunate and happy for the remainder of his life.

Well, the bard's romantic wish, for the accomplishment of which he was prepared to travel over the entire surface of the globe, was realised in my case, at least so far as obtaining a specimen of the magic plant is concerned. Nor was I looking for it at the time. On the contrary, I was merely gathering wild flowers when I came upon and secured a specimen of the four-leafed shamrock itself.

Ever since that auspicious moment I have been awaiting the advent of the extra happiness and good fortune that my precious possession is to bring me. In fact I am living in a state of perpetual suspense, like Sidney Smith's description of a "young clergyman distantly related to a bishop." Of course I know that the good luck must come sooner or later, but occasional doubts will arise, suggesting that it is stopping over long upon the way. In the meanwhile I may occupy myself by describing other kindred plants in Uruguay.

There are many trefoils to be met with, all of them closely allied to each other, and to the shamrock from which I plucked my treasure, though differing from it in some essential respects. The most common, and at the same time the brightest and most showy, of them I will call the mid-winter primrose, from the time of the year at which its blossoms make their appearance, and their strong resemblance to our own favourite spring flower. They are, however, less delicate in shade, being more of a bright sulphur-yellow.

Here I may mention that, in Uruguay, winter lacks much of the conventional character of desolation with which we, in northern latitudes, are accustomed to associate it. It is true that there the clouds occasionally open their sluice-gates and pour down torrents of rain upon the thirsty earth, which has grown brown and parched by summer droughts, until the rivers flood the districts through which they flow, so that the eye grows weary of the waste of waters stretched out before it. But when the floods subside, the desolate scene is replaced with marvellous rapidity by a rich green growth of grass sprinkled everywhere with flowers peculiar to the season.

In addition to the mid-winter primrose, two other trefoils then blossom forth with similarly-shaped flowers, but differing in colour, one of them being white and the other pink.

The normal number of petals of all three, as in the case of our own primrose, is five, but in this respect both they and it present many examples with great variety of numbers.

There is another little trefoil common enough in Uruguay, the blossom of which is yellow in colour, and very minute, but differently shaped, being somewhat like that of the ordinary clover.

I sometimes think that it was a pity Saint Patrick did not meet with it, and select it as an emblem for his beloved country. Upon each of its leaves is impressed a small but perfectly-shaped heart in a rich chocolate-colour, on a deep green ground. It would perhaps be more explicit were I to adopt the phraseology of the kennel to express my meaning, and describe it as a liver-coloured heart; but the association of ideas suggested by the composite term is rather too anatomical for my purpose.

It appears to me that the trefoil in question would represent Hibernian peculiarities more suitably and neatly than the ordinary shamrock does. Its softer and brighter green corresponds more closely with the verdant appearance of the isle itself, while the shrinking nature of the plant would convey a delicate intimation of the modest and retiring side of the Irish character, too often overlooked by those who criticise us. Then, I may add, what better emblem could possibly be found for a land where hearts are always trumps, than that which bears upon its leaves the effigy of a human heart, an organ conventionally accepted as being the source of man's warmest and most susceptible qualities?

It is now too late, I fear, to suggest a change of emblems, with any hope of its being generally adopted. If Saint Patrick had not been in such a hurry, all might yet be satisfactorily arranged in this respect; but Irishmen, whether saints or sinners, are always too much inclined to be impetuous.

Of course I cannot but be aware that in treating Saint Patrick as being unquestionably an Irishman by birth, I am falling foul of the fond aspirations of those enthusiastic Scots who would like to claim him as a countryman of their own, and of the historians who assert that he was born in Gaul, and brought over captive to Ireland by that celebrated warrior, "Niall of the Nine Hostages," who sold the future saint into slavery in Armagh for the price of a yearling calf. As regards the claim of the Scotchmen, I don't blame them in the least degree for striving to associate Saint Patrick with Saint Andrew in the responsibilities of the position of patron saint and representative of their country. I grant them, too, that the Irish were first called Scots, and whatever advantage they can derive from that they are justly entitled to; but with every wish to oblige our neighbours in all reasonable matters, I cannot bring myself to willingly resign to them our national saint.

Looking next to the pretensions set up on

behalf of Gaul, they rest in my opinion upon an unphilosophical treatment of the historical element in the question. The contention appears to be that because the youth, who afterwards became the saint, was found in Gaul, he must, therefore, have been born there. This is a clear case of *non sequitur*. If you find that curiosity "a fly in amber," it by no means follows that the insect was born in the interior of the solid in which it has been discovered imbedded.

The fact is worthy of consideration, that there was a considerable amount of intercourse between Ireland and Gaul, and many other parts of the continent of Europe, at and before the period to which our speculations relate. Did not the celebrated Irish warrior, Carausius, a County Wexford man, become Roman Emperor? And if we read the history of our country carefully, we shall find that Irish monarchs and soldiers of fortune of those times were perpetually leading military expeditions into Gaul and elsewhere. It may, therefore, well be the case that the future Saint Patrick, when a boy, accompanied one of them as page, or in some other honourable capacity, and that he was captured and left behind, to be subsequently recaptured and brought back to Ireland by " Niall of the Nine Hostages," who, with that aptitude for business transactions for which he was celebrated, turned him at once into ready money.

I will only refer to one other circumstance which seems to me to point strongly to Ireland as the place of Saint Patrick's birth. It is but natural that any man, and especially a saint, should love his native country above all others. Did not Saint Patrick, I would ask, show extra affection for Ireland in banishing from her shores both snakes and toads for ever, while he pronounced no similar interdict, as far as history records, against them either in Gaul or Caledonia?

CHAPTER XV

THE SNAKE IN THE GRASS

Latet anguis in herbâ, so runs the Latin proverb; and perhaps a well-bred snake that knows what is expected of it, and acts up to its responsibilities, does usually lie concealed in the grass. Nor have I any great personal objection to the habit, provided I happen to be wearing long boots when I come across one. But if the classical authority is correct in this matter, then all I can say is, that I must have mixed in anything but good serpentine society, for those I have met, and their name is legion, were by no means always hidden away in the grass. They frequently appeared to wish for no concealment whatever, but, on the contrary, were inclined to make their presence both known and felt, and that, too, in awkward places, and at the most inconvenient times. If I were called upon to express an opinion in the matter, it would be to the effect that nowhere are you so likely to meet with them as where you least expect to do so.

For example, who would think a biscuit-box or a teapot a probable place in which to find a living specimen of the kind? And yet they have been known to try a temporary residence in both these places. I would appeal to any qualified judge in the matter to say whether it is "good form" for a snake to insist upon making a morning call in your bedroom, just at the critical moment when you are in your bath, and wholly unprepared for the reception of strangers. I have an unpleasant recollection of a visit of the kind. What made matters more uncomfortable was that the unbidden guest did not come alone, but in company with a great, lumbering, ill-visaged toad, with which it affected to be having a game of romps, though I am inclined to think that it meant the sport to end in breakfast. I confess the reception I gave that snake was not of a nature to encourage the cultivation of any closer intimacy between us, or characterised by any high appreciation of the duties of hospitality, and it left in a hurry.

When I turned round to attend to the toad, which had been momentarily overlooked in the more animated interview with the snake, it flopped clumsily into the bath, just as if it did not know where it was going. Here was an aggravation to my annoyance, and I called my servant to aid me. He was an Irishman, long resident in South America, yet still retained a fresh and fervent hatred of snakes and toads that would have done credit to Saint Patrick himself in olden times. The expression he made use of, however, when he took in the position of affairs was anything but saintly. He was a man of resources, and after the first outburst he said, " Wait, sir, till I lasso him." In a very short time he returned with a piece of fine cord and a loop at the end of it, with which he dexterously entangled the toad, and carried it off in triumph.

It is a wonderful country for the use of the lasso; nearly everything is done there by its aid. I almost believe that if a dentist in South America had to extract a tooth, he would begin the operation by lassoing the patient.

That snakes eat toads I have had frequent

opportunities of learning from my own observation, having often witnessed the pursuit, the capture, and the repast. Once I came across the dead body of a snake which had been cut in two upon the railway by a passing train, and in its mouth, still held fast, was a toad, also dead.

One of our engineers had an experience connected with a bath and a snake which I may narrate here, though it throws my own story that I have given above somewhat into the shade, inasmuch as it includes the additional fact that the intelligence of a dog is strikingly exhibited by it. The engineer in question was returning from taking a bath, and walking along a pathway on which his dog was lying down. When my friend got close to the spot, instead of the affectionate reception he was accustomed to, he was met by a savage growl, followed by a sharp, angry bark, indicating the determination of the dog to bar the passage. Looking about him in surprise for some explanation of this extraordinary conduct on the part of an animal whose usual manners were perfect of their kind, he discovered a large snake lying in the path, just before him. Thereupon he retreated cautiously, and having procured a stick, returned to settle the disputed "right of way" with the snake, which he killed. When this was accomplished, but not till then, the dog's demeanour changed, and he gave vent to his natural feelings, explaining as well as he could the cause of his previous strange behaviour, and exhibiting in an unmistakable manner his delight at the escape of his master from a danger so imminent.

As a general rule, one only makes the acquaintance of individual snakes at a time, though we do read of their being met with occasionally in the Western States of North America coiled up together in great numbers, in the form of a pyramid. Exceptional circumstances, however, gave me the opportunity of seeing a great many of them in one locality in Uruguay. A valley, in which there was much thick brushwood and coarse grass, and known to be a favourite haunt of snakes, was suddenly flooded, so that they had to swim to dry land in search of new quarters. While thus engaged I saw numbers of them in the water, apparently well able to take care of themselves, and swimming strongly.

The result of this migration of the snakes was

that the rock embankments of the railway and its broken stone ballast in that locality became thickly inhabited by a colony of them, which made one careful how he picked his steps when walking along the line, as at least two kinds of the snakes to be met with there were venomous. If so, it is only fair to them to state that we lost no men from snake bites, and only one man on the railway works died from the bite of a toad. When my Irish servant told me of his death I inquired the cause of the fatality, and received the characteristic reply, " A frog bit him."

CHAPTER XVI

LAW AND LAWYERS

MANY people find occupation in wondering how it happens that legal proceedings, which are designed to keep matters working in a straight and even groove, where injustice should find no place, so frequently produce results exactly the reverse of what they are intended to accomplish.

The explanation of this appears plain enough, if one will only take the trouble to look for it in the right place.

Why start by tying a bandage over the eyes of Justice, and then expect her to see all the more clearly for it, just as if she were a "thought-reader" intent upon finding a pin hidden away in some very unusual cushion? How can she possibly know when some weight has been put into one of the scales she holds so fairly balanced in her hand, in order to bring it down unduly? Depend upon it, many of the miscarriages of justice, and the wrongs committed by her representatives, in her name, are due to her bandaged eyes in the game of legal "blind man's buff."

South America presents a wide field for investigating the curious problems that so often arise out of legal proceedings. The growth of lawyers there somewhat resembles the ordinary vegetation of the country in its tropical profusion, and the similitude extends to the rank legal weeds sometimes to be met with. These tend at times to choke and conceal the purer and more wholesome vegetation.

It is a pity that such should be the case, as I have met with many excellent men connected with the law in South America who would reflect credit upon any country. It must not be forgotten that it is not about such as they are, but about exceptional members of the legal profession, that I am now writing. My personal experience of this latter class is scarcely of sufficient importance to be recalled, except as exhibiting a phase of the matter that is not without interest.

Some of these peculiar people to whom I have referred endeavoured to organise opposition to the railway on the part of the landowners, that gave us a good deal of trouble. Others went about among our workmen and sub-contractors, inquiring whether they had any complaints to make of us, and generously offering, if they had, to take legal proceedings against us on their behalf, free of cost to the claimant.

One sub-contractor, who was doing his work so badly that we were obliged to take it out of his hands and finish it ourselves, listened to the persuasion of a philanthropic lawyer of the kind I have described, and made large demands upon us for damages. The strange part of the business was, that the contractor's excuse for the manner in which his work was done had previously been that his prices were too low, and consequently he could not afford to do any better, as he was losing heavily by his contract.

But when the lawsuit began it changed the whole aspect of affairs, for it then appeared that his anticipated profits, which he had been prevented realising, amounted to even more than the total estimated cost of the works he had undertaken to complete. This was a curious circumstance, which I thought would of itself be sufficient to dispose of the matter.

But in this I was mistaken, as the judge did not appear to think it strange that a part should be greater than the whole, notwithstanding Euclid's opinion to the contrary. The lawsuit dragged its slow length along from month to month, and we were threatened with all manner of pains and penalties, the least of which was an application for an injunction to prevent the railway being opened for traffic until the case was settled. Matters looked very gloomy, and while still in this condition the judge before whom the case was proceeding required further proof on some point from our opponent.

This gave great offence. His lawyer rushed into print, and published a violent letter in the local newspaper, taxing the judge with corruption, and boldly asserting that he had been bribed (contempt of court does not appear to have reached that region yet). Our lawyer was delighted; he rubbed his hands with glee, and said the case was as good as won for us. Nor was he far wrong in his opinion, for shortly afterwards overtures for a settlement were made by the opposite side, which resulted in their accepting, as payment in full, the amount we had been prepared to lodge in court at the opening of the trial, as the balance due to the contractor on account of the works executed by him up to the time when they had been taken out of his hands.

I subsequently heard that this settlement gave rise to a new complication between the lawyer and his client, as the former not only absorbed the whole of the money we paid, but demanded more, what he had received being, he said, insufficient to pay his costs.

But it is necessary to go beyond the confines of Uruguay to other parts of South America if we desire to study the subject of law and lawyers on a larger and higher scale.

An extraordinary and suggestive case occurred in a neighbouring republic in the year 1892.

A farmer, in a lonely situation, with no one but his wife living in the house with him, sold some cattle one evening to a dealer who was passing by. That night there was a knock at his door, and when it was opened two men with blackened faces rushed in, and demanded the money received for the cattle. The farmer was a plucky fellow, and gave a flat refusal to the request, whereupon the robbers tied him up and threatened to kill him. His frightened wife pleaded for her husband, and offered to show where the money was hidden if only they would spare his life. This proposition being agreed to, one man mounted guard over his prisoner, while the other accompanied the woman into the bedroom to get the money. There she placed the candle on a table, and opened a chest containing clothes to look for the object of her search.

It proved, however, to be of a very different kind to what the robbers expected.

She laid hold of a loaded revolver, with which she shot the man who had accompanied her to the room, and when his companion, hearing the noise, rushed to the door and saw what had happened, and that the woman had got him carefully covered with the weapon she had shown herself so expert in using, he fled from the house in dismay. The courageous wife then set free her husband, and they prepared to resist another attack, expecting that the man who escaped would return with a stronger party during the night-time. But they were not further molested, and when the neighbours and police visited the scene next morning, it was discovered that the dead body lying in the house was that of the attorney-general of the district.

One of the newspapers headed its comments on the affair with the title of "A nice thing in Attorney-Generals," while another publicly expressed the opinion that the robber who had escaped was most probably a judge of the criminal court.

This was certainly a strange development, for in the present day one does not expect to find prominent officers of justice emulating the historic exploits of Dick Turpin and his brotherhood of the road.

More recently a curious case, also unconnected with Uruguay, arose out of ordinary law proceedings; not amateur acting like the example previously cited, but a regular performance upon the ordinary legal stage. I am obliged to admit, however, that one of the actors in it belonged to my own profession.

It was the case of a railway which crossed some swampy land in a remote district, taking a portion of it that was valued by experts in the usual way. But the price they put upon it did not satisfy the owner, and the matter went to legal arbitration.

The company's representative was willing to give double the valuation in order to settle the question out of court, but the landowner's arbitrator stood out for between two and three hundred times the valuation. An engineer was called in to act as umpire, and he fixed the price at about one hundred times the value placed upon the land by the original experts.

Against this decision the railway company appealed to the court, but the judge confirmed it. The peculiarities of the transaction were stated by a newspaper commenting upon it to be, that the nominal proprietor and his arbitrator were subsequently discovered to be partners in the ownership of the land, while the judge who decided the case was a third partner, and the paper added that the umpire laboured under strong public suspicion of being a fourth.

I knew of a railway which at one part of its length passed through an extensive property that, at the time I mention, was before the court for the purpose of having the succession to it formally declared. There were so many heirs who laid claim to an interest in it, that the difficulty of deciding between them, or apportioning the relative shares in which they were entitled to inherit it, appears to have quite surpassed the judge's arithmetical powers, so he was said to have hit upon the simpler expedient of throwing over the claimants altogether, and divided the property between himself and an individual high in power.

Another curious case came to my knowledge incidentally. I was sitting reading in my room in a hotel in a remote district one night, when I heard a knock at the door, which was then opened, and in walked an officer, who gave me a polite message from the governor of an adjoining province in a neighbouring republic, who also happened to be there at the time, and, hearing of my presence, politely sent to ask me to come in and have coffee with him. Upon entering his room I found a number of gentlemen collected there. The conversation was of a general character, but it was easy to see it was no ordinary social gathering, and that the object of their meeting must relate to some business of importance. I therefore remained but a short time with the assembled company, and then took my departure, leaving them to proceed with the work they had in hand, of which I subsequently discovered the nature.

A claim to establish a right to a very large tract of land had been before the court for years, without any prospect of a settlement being arrived at. In fact, the lawsuit was said to have been an heirloom in the family of the claimant, handed down from father to son, until it came to the representative in the present generation. He was one of those philosophical people believing in the maxim that "half a loaf is better than no bread," and it was said he endeavoured to convert some influential persons to his views in this respect.

There are people who seem to be able to command success, and he was one of them. Justice, that had been sleeping soundly for many previous generations, suddenly awoke, and decided the lawsuit in his favour, and the gentlemen whom I had seen at the hotel were met together to arrange the necessary proceedings for giving effect to the decree of court. The result was the wholesale eviction of a district as large as an Irish county.

Indulging in peculiar legal practice, however, occasionally gets one into trouble, and sometimes into something else. I remember hearing of a judge who tried the game once too often, and as a consequence, became himself the inmate of a prison, to which he had in his time consigned many a delinquent.

CHAPTER XVII

AMATEUR DIPLOMACY

"One never knows what he can do till he tries" is a trite but true saying. His capabilities may lie hidden and undiscovered by casual observers, and even unsuspected by himself, until the divining rod of necessity upon being applied indicates their existence and nature. I have not served in the "foreign office," nor studied in the school that teaches the chief use of words is to conceal one's thoughts, and yet, when brought face to face with a diplomatic difficulty—and I have had to enter the lists without being encased in the usual educational armour for protection in an encounter of the kind—I think I may, without undue boasting, claim to have been fairly successful.

One day a man of ours went into the town of Santa Ana do Libramento, in Brazil, with a couple of saddled horses for the use of engineers who were stopping at the hotel there. After he had passed the police barracks he heard a whistle, and upon looking round saw a policeman, who said he wanted to speak to him. Our man replied he would come back in a moment, when he had left the horses at the hotel, to which he pointed, a few yards farther on in the street. This he did, but on his way back, instead of going straight to the police office he most improperly stopped at a shop to buy a packet of cigarettes. While so engaged the policeman entered and demanded why he had not stopped at once when first accosted. An angry altercation ensued, and the policeman drew his sword, which our man wrested from him and threw away. The representative of law and order next produced his revolver, but was speedily disarmed of this weapon also, and it shared the fate of the sword.

At this stage of the proceedings some other policemen came running up, and separated the combatants. They then arrested our man and took him to the barracks, where he was brought up at once before the officer in charge. The first thing done was to search him, when, fortunately, he was found to have no weapon of any kind about him. The officer then demanded what he meant by trying to murder the policeman, and drawing his sword, gave the prisoner a severe cut with it across the head and arm, following up the attack by a thrust which the intended victim avoided by springing hastily aside.

In the meanwhile his master, who was the engineer in charge of the adjoining district of the railway, and resided close by, called at the police office, saw the officer, and expressed his regret for any misconduct his servant had been guilty of, and offered at the same time to give satisfactory bail for his appearance when called upon, if they would let him out in order that his wounds might be dressed. This request was rudely refused, and our engineer was turned out of the office; but later in the day the man was set free, and no subsequent proceedings were taken against him.

I laid the case before her Majesty's minister at Montevideo, a most accomplished and obliging gentleman, who at once undertook to have the matter properly represented to the Brazilian Government at Rio de Janeiro. For this purpose he required the sworn depositions of the Brazilian people who had been spectators of the scene.

These latter, although strong in their denunciation of the action of the police at the time, were afraid to put their testimony in writing, saying they should be marked down for subsequent injury if they did so. Lacking these necessary documents, regular diplomacy could not be put in motion, so that we were thrown back upon our own resources. We had a large intercourse with Brazil at the time, and were in the habit of buying a considerable quantity of timber and other materials for the construction of the railway there, and I feared if we allowed the matter to drop the police would consider themselves privileged to treat our people with scant consideration, which might place us in a very awkward position at times. I therefore adopted the course I thought most likely to bring them to a more rational frame of mind. I issued orders that no person employed upon our railway works in Uruguay should cross the frontier of Brazil, and that no further purchases of material should be made there. This, as I anticipated it would, produced immense dissatisfaction. Several merchants and others begged me to withdraw the order; but I was obdurate, and refused to do so. I made it clear to them that we were obliged to protect ourselves against a recurrence of such treatment as we had already received at the hands of the police.

Different people volunteered to negotiate an arrangement of the difficulty between us and Brazil, but I declined the offer of their good offices, and refused to enter into any negotiations until I had received a written apology from the authorities.

When this unsatisfactory position of affairs had lasted for some time, there came to me one day an officer with whom I was well acquainted, and told me he was closely related to the general commanding upon the southern frontier of Brazil. He explained that his relative was very much annoyed at what had happened, and most anxious to put an end to the unfriendly feeling existing at the time. For this purpose he desired to know what would satisfy me, so as to withdraw my prohibition, and allow matters to resume the original condition which they occupied before the dispute arose.

My demand required a written apology, expressing regret for the occurrence, and an undertaking that nothing of the kind should happen again; the public reprimand and punishment of the officer who had attacked and wounded an unarmed prisoner, also of the policeman with whom the quarrel originated; and lastly, the issuing of explicit orders that all persons employed upon the railway were to be treated with due regard to what is customary in similar cases among civilised nations.

These terms were at once agreed to, and I am bound to say were carried out in no grudging or slipshod manner. Even more than I had asked for was conceded: the policemen of the station were all removed to the interior and replaced by new men, and matters upon the frontier, so far as concerned us, worked well and smoothly for the remainder of the time occupied in the construction of the railway.

On another occasion I had a somewhat perplexing experience in overcoming a diplomatic difficulty. The engineers and other members of the staff had been working very willingly and hard, early and late, and I thought in recognition of this satisfactory condition of affairs I would give them a dinner at Christmas time in the hotel. My intention was to restrict the guests to those who were employed upon the railway, but this was frustrated by the civility of a friend. He was the colonel of a cavalry regiment quartered in the town where we were to dine, and, upon hearing of our intended festivity, he begged to be allowed to send his band, which was a very good one, to play for us on the occasion. His kindly proposal could not well be declined without the danger of giving offence, which it was particularly desirable to avoid. Having accepted the offer, I had, of course, to ask the colonel himself to make one of the party, explaining at the same time the strictly private nature of the entertainment, to which, had it been a public one, we would have extended the invitations to his officers also.

It then became necessary to ask the chief civilian of the place, the *Gefe Politico*, for fear of creating jealousy.

Upon the day of our festivities we met at the hotel, a party of about twenty-four. Everything went well until we came to that critical stage of the proceedings, the introduction of the toasts. At this point I explained to my neighbours on the right and left of me, who represented the civil and military powers, that our universal custom on occasions of the kind was to propose the health of her Majesty Queen Victoria as the first item on the programme of our festive oratory.

This suggestion they took very seriously, and after a brief consultation, they informed me they should have to leave the table if the health of the President of the Republic was not the first toast proposed. I appealed ineffectually to their feelings upon the principle of *place aux dames*. I next urged the fact that it was practically a British gathering, and the room, having been hired for the evening, might be considered to be British territory for the moment; but their views on international law would not take them so far as to admit the correctness of my contention.

The reader may, perhaps, fancy that the solution of the difficulty was as obvious as it was simple, and entirely in my own hands. All that was necessary was to have no speeches of any kind that evening. Such a course would have been wholly inapplicable; for one might as well have a dinner of the kind without eatables or wine, as without toasts when the Spanish element was present.

As a last resource I explained to our official guests that I thought they were just a little too careful of the dignity of the ruler of the Republic, in forbidding a custom that I had been allowed to follow on similar occasions in foreign countries on the continent of Europe. This softened their hearts, and they withdrew all further opposition to the course I proposed adopting. They drank her Majesty's health enthusiastically, cheered lustily, and joined us in singing "God save the Queen." Immediately following this display of loyalty I proposed the health of the President of the Republic, who, I felt assured, had he been one of the party on that occasion, would have been the first to stand aside and make way for her Majesty. It is just possible that, in gratitude for having been allowed to carry my point, I described the character of the first magistrate of the State rather as it should have been than as it actually was; for, upon reflection, I could not help thinking that I struck a key somewhat too high for the general "concert pitch" of South American rulers. Be this as it may, good feeling was perfectly restored, and I believe my own health was proposed at least half-a-dozen times that evening. On each of these occasions I was found to possess some new and excellent quality previously undiscovered by my most intimate acquaintances.

"All's well that ends well" we are told, and we may apply the remark to our festivities on that evening.

It is true my satisfaction with the result has been somewhat modified by the assurance I have since received from an experienced diplomatist, that I was altogether wrong, and guilty of a breach of international etiquette in insisting upon the Queen's health being proposed first in a foreign country. It may be so. As I explained at the beginning of this chapter, I had not been brought up in the devious ways of diplomacy, but, all the same, whether right or wrong, under similar circumstances, I think I would act again as I did before.

CHAPTER XVIII

PEN VERSUS SWORD

"The pen is mightier than the sword" says the enthusiastic journalist, giving publicity to a popular proverb that is a product of the northern hemisphere, not, for so far, as well acclimatised in South America as the friends of that continent could desire.

For example, what would the unfortunate newspaper editor have to say about it, while smarting from the 309 lashes administered to him by order of an irate colonel whose conduct he had been rash enough to criticise in his paper?

It is true the military gentleman, when asked by the civil power for an explanation of the circumstance, excused himself on the plea that it was all a mistake of orders on the part of the sergeant to whom he had issued them. Whether the poor editor found the explanation entirely satisfactory does not appear, but I think he must have acknowledged to himself that in his case at all events the proverb did not hold good.

There is something curious in the number of the lashes too; why the extra nine? Perhaps the colonel had some superstitious belief in the luck that lurks in odd numbers, following the example of our old friend Rory O'More in the song.

The editorial experience, however, did not happen in Uruguay, but much farther north, where the temperature, the temper, politics, and things generally are much warmer than in the River Plate.

It is not so very long ago, if report be true, that other curious methods were adopted in South America for dealing with refractory editors. One of this class having given offence to those in power by the freedom of his criticisms, was arrested and confined in a narrow passage between the cages of two jaguars, notorious for their bad tempers, coupled with an intense dislike to the society of men.

The intervening space was so regulated that neither of the ferocious animals could get its paws quite so far as the middle line between the cages, so that a spare, active person, if very careful to follow the classical advice, *in medio tutissimus ibis*, might manage to pass without receiving any injury, though the achievement would be both exciting and dangerous. But what made the matter still more cruel in this particular case was that the unfortunate editor happened to be very stout, and therefore the more easily reached by the occupants of the cages. Adding insult to injury, he was handed a chair on which to sit, and furnished at the same time with a copy of his own paper, that had brought him into trouble, in order that he might read and meditate upon its contents during his exciting imprisonment. People, jesting about the matter afterwards, which seemed very heartless, said that the tailor had a rare job repairing the editor's torn clothes when he got out.

It is probable that this is one of the stories that require to be seasoned with many grains of salt, although an old soldier assured me that, when on guard where the wild animals were kept, he had frequently seen opponents of the Government of the day meet with a worse fate than that which befell the stout editor.

There was a trial of strength between the pen and sword, which I remember, that caused considerable excitement at the time in the locality where it occurred. A series of fierce attacks was made in a newspaper upon the colonel of a certain regiment, charging him with gross cruelty to those under his command, besides numerous other crimes of a varied and sensational character. That which appeared to be the most startling was that he had occasionally sentenced men to as many as twelve thousand lashes! If the culprits possessed the proverbial nine lives of the animal which gives its name to the instrument of torture from the lashes of which they were condemned to suffer, they would have lost them all long before the full sentence had been carried out.

An additional complaint made against the colonel was, that when his victims had been flogged to death he would not allow them to be buried in consecrated ground, but had their bodies cast into holes dug in the river's bank to receive them, with as little ceremony as would be used in burying the carcass of a dog or cat.

What a commentary is this upon the stirring ballad of "The Bold Soldier Boy," in which that illustrious warrior, Mickey Free, sang the praises of a military life! One thing is quite certain, that the lot of the South American "Tommy Atkins" is far less happy than that depicted in the verses alluded to.

For a long time the colonel treated the newspaper attacks with contempt; but in the end the scandal became so public, that an investigation was ordered, which resulted in his being relieved of his command and relegated to private life in supposed disgrace. I use the qualifying expression, as many people boldly, and persistently, asserted that confidential relations between him and the Government continued to exist.

While the colonel in question was under the cloud of public disapprobation, and smarting from the loss of his regiment, a friend of mine, who knew him intimately, heard his version of the story, which was narrated to me afterwards. "I did flog the man to death," he said, referring to one particular case, "but what else could I do? He had committed several murders before he came to me, and he was beginning at his old tricks again. I knew it was useless to hand him over to the civil arm for punishment, as he would only be sent back to me for promotion after a while. I had to settle the matter myself, and the twelve thousand lashes did it." In truth there is much force in what the colonel said when put in another form. It is impossible to keep up the discipline of a regiment when its ranks are largely recruited from among the criminal inmates of the gaols, a practice all too common in South America.

And yet there is something to be said upon the other side to account for its adoption. The life of a murderer, when he has been convicted, seems to be held as particularly precious in that long-suffering land. It shocks the public moral sense to think that a bloodthirsty criminal, whom nothing can reclaim, should be executed, while the cruel fate of his victims arouses but a passing sympathy.

This forbearing attitude towards the law-breaking classes would naturally produce the undesirable result of gaols full to overflowing, and very costly to maintain, but for the expedient which is frequently resorted to of allowing the inmates to volunteer to serve as soldiers. Such undesirable recruits join their regiments with the intention of deserting upon the first favourable opportunity, as shown by a case of the kind conducted upon a wholesale scale, which was mentioned in the chapter on the "Haunt of the Outlaw." In the meantime, while serving with the colours, they are always ready and willing to keep their hands in practice at their original trade, when a chance of doing so presents itself. Under such circumstances, one can easily understand how difficult it is for an officer in command of a corps so recruited to keep his men in order.

The pen having conquered the sword in the contest I have narrated, its wielder, while flushed with victory, laid about him on every side with immense energy. He attacked many persons, holding them up to public odium, one of them being an important government official, who also in the end was superseded; but whether or not this was due to the newspaper attacks, I cannot say.

Here again the editor was certainly sufficiently outspoken to satisfy the strongest advocate of candour in the treatment of public men, and the discussion of their actions; but before long an attempt was made to check his reforming ardour

By this time the enterprising censor of public officials and of others had stirred up a considerable amount of enmity. He was pretty much in the position of an intruding bluebottle in a hornets' nest, when it has disturbed all the inmates by its buzzing, and will not let them rest. One night as he left the café which he was in the habit of frequenting he was met at the door by a man, who fired at him point-blank with a revolver, to which the editor replied in similar style, whereupon a contest of small-arms ensued, and continued until all the ammunition on both sides was expended, with the curious result that although some dozen shots had been fired, neither of the combatants was anything the worse for the encounter. The only sufferer was a poor stray dog that happened to be passing by at the time, and had the misfortune to get in the way of one of the ill-directed bullets. The aggressor on this occasion, when arrested, proved to have influential friends, and very little was done to him for the double crime of shooting the dog and firing at the editor.

After this incident the newspaper attacks became still more bitter, as was not at all surprising; but before long the editor announced his intention of moving from the locality, as he did not find it healthy.

Here we may take leave of him, but a subsequent occurrence in the same town reminds one of him incidentally, as it refers to an episode very similar to his impromptu duel.

There had been a change made in the whole staff of government officials in the district, and the new second in command, not long after his appointment, was attacked one night in the public street by two men wearing disguises. He defended himself pluckily, but received some very severe knife wounds, from which, however, he recovered. One of his assailants was identified, and proved to be related to some one of importance, as happened in the similar case previously quoted; but I do not remember to have heard that any punishment was meted out to him either.

CHAPTER XIX

RIVERA AND SANTA ANA

IN a previous chapter, near the beginning of this volume, we paid a hurried visit to Rivera, the town of many "first officials," and I now propose to take my readers there once more, in order that they may become better acquainted with it, as well as with its Brazilian neighbour, Santa Ana do Libramento.

These twin towns lie upon the frontier between the two republics, and are separated only by a neutral zone or belt 110 yards wide, on which no buildings are erected.

In this "no man's land" there stands a high hill, from the top of which an extensive view of the surrounding district can be obtained. Besides being useful as a post of observation for both countries as to what their neighbours are about, it has interesting geological features, being traversed by a huge trap-dyke.

At its base there is a bountiful spring of good drinking water, and at no great distance to the west is the source of the river Cuñapiru, which, in the lower part of its course, before joining the Tacuarembó Grande, of which it is a tributary, flows through the goldfields of Uruguay.

Rivera, which has a population of about 1400, is situated 352 miles to the north of Montevideo, measured along the line of railway that now connects them. The road into it from the south crosses the above-mentioned Cuñapiru by a small bridge, at which there is a toll-bar. The collector who levied payment at it, and his wife, corresponded, in one respect, to the theory of that close observer of human nature, Mr. Weller, senior, as regards the class of people who take to keeping toll-bars, or pikes, as he called them. They had met with serious disappointments in life; in fact, their history was a very sad and pathetic one, and it was that which caused them to adopt the calling in which I made their acquaintance. So far Mr. Weller was perfectly right, but his further proposition, that it was because people became misanthropical that they took to keeping toll-bars, in order to revenge themselves upon mankind, was utterly wrong in this instance, for a kinder or more hospitable couple than those I am writing of it would not be easy to meet with. When our surveying party first reached Rivera these good people insisted upon our dismounting and entering their house, where they regaled us with cherry-brandy. Nor was it on this occasion only that they did so; each time we passed the toll-bar the hospitality was repeated.

Now, however popular cherry-brandy may be upon the sideboard, at a hunting breakfast, in our cold northern climate on a damp winter's morning, it is not the most suitable or cooling of drinks on the frontier of Brazil, with the thermometer at 100° Fahr. in the shade. For this reason, and not wishing to offend these kind and hospitable people, some of us, in order to escape from the dilemma thus arising, frequently risked a ducking by riding across the river at another place where the ford was uncertain. Nor can our enemies assert that by so doing we saved paying toll, for by that time we had contracted with the toll-keeper for a monthly payment to cover all our horses and people.

The chief trade of Rivera is said to have been of

a contraband nature; but this industry received a serious check from the shooting of two of its most vigorous adherents by the police in skirmishes on the frontier, when we were there. One frequently hears allusions on both sides of the boundary line to the fact of some article having been brought in " under the poncho," which is the local metaphor to intimate that it was smuggled in. I have even heard the expression used with reference to a piano, an instrument altogether too large and cumbrous to be concealed beneath a poncho, in the literal sense.

The most attractive spot about Rivera was an old garden full of magnificent orange-trees; but it is otherwise bare and uninteresting, although both soil and climate are suitable to the growth of many rare plants.

In a garden at Rivera, while walking one day with the owner, I was startled to hear a savage growl from some wild animal quite close to me. Upon asking for an explanation I was taken to an iron cage, which had been concealed from our view by the thick foliage that intervened. In it was the finest specimen of a young jaguar that I had ever seen. Though not full grown, his coat was beautifully marked. But the manner in which he received all overtures of friendship from strangers was not calculated to encourage one to persist in the attempt to gain his good will. No doubt he may have inherited infirmities of temper that were not improved by imprisonment.

The Brazilian town of Santa Ana do Libramento, which lies to the north of Rivera, is an old established settlement, with about 1700 inhabitants. One meets everywhere evidence of its age in the fine orange-trees with which its gardens abound.

It, too, has only a small legitimate trade, but all that is necessary to make both towns prosperous and important places is the establishment of a well-organised custom-house at the frontier. If this were done, and the corresponding regulations framed upon a wise and liberal basis, it would greatly foster the growth of international commerce at this point.

It is understood that the Governments of both countries recognise the importance of the matter, so that it is to be hoped a favourable solution of the question may ere long be arrived at.

One of the engineers engaged upon the construction of the railway met with a serious accident at Rivera. He was in the act of dismounting from his horse when his revolver fell to the ground and a cartridge went off, the bullet passing through his leg and imbedding itself in the door-frame of the house he was about to enter.

A Brazilian surgeon from Santa Ana was called in, who examined and bandaged up the wounded limb. Everything went on well from day to day, and the patient was rapidly regaining his usual health, the wound being almost healed, when the surgeon in attendance said it would be necessary to have an operation, and cut down to the bone to see if it had sustained any injury. My friend asked for an explanation of this extraordinary proposal, as he was not suffering any pain, nor was there any symptom from the first to indicate that the bone had been touched by the bullet. The surgeon admitted these facts, but stuck to his point that the operation was necessary, as it would clear away any possible doubt about the matter. Besides, in performing it he could then get the assistance of another eminent surgeon, which might not be obtained so easily at another time. Thereupon the wounded man said quietly,

"If an operation must be performed, I shall go to Montevideo and have it done in the British hospital there." This was quite another way of looking at the matter, and the doctor agreed to have a consultation the next day about it. He did so, and the conclusion arrived at was that an operation was unnecessary after all, an opinion the correctness of which subsequent experience corroborated.

At the hotel in Santa Ana I had a narrow escape on one occasion of being asphyxiated. Mosquitoes were very bad at the time, and a waiter gave me a pastille, which he told me to burn when I went to bed, and that it would drive them all away. I followed his directions, with unexpected results.

Not long after I had gone to sleep I awoke suffocating, and to my horror found myself unable to get up, or call for help. I could move my arms, however, so I got hold of the candlestick and struck with it against the door of the next room, which was fortunately within reach of my bed.

This awoke two friends of mine, who came in to see what was wrong, and when they had thrown open door and windows, I soon recovered the power of speech and the use of my limbs. Since then I have been very careful not to try fancy methods for getting rid of mosquitoes.

Life upon the frontier has its own little excitements, as, for example, the shooting of contrabandists, to which allusion has been already made. Nor are these exponents of "free trade" always the only people to suffer in encounters of the kind; they frequently retaliate with considerable effect. It is no rare occurrence when near the frontier to have one's rest disturbed by the report of firearms discharged in the preventive service.

But it is during political commotions that the fun becomes both fast and furious. At such times dwellers near the boundary line have the doubtful advantage of a double supply of excitement of the kind, that furnished by the inhabitants of both countries. Practically it makes little difference whether it is Uruguayan or Brazilian bullets that are flying about.

When fighting takes place between Government troops and insurgents near the frontier, if the revolutionists are the beaten side they invariably seek refuge on foreign soil. On such occasions their opponents seldom fail to favour them with a parting *feu de joie* of ball cartridge, continuing the salute until those in retreat have penetrated farther into the asylum of a friendly territory than a rifle bullet will carry.

Sticklers for the rights of neutrality may look upon this as a breach of the code which should regulate such matters, but in South America an act of the kind is seldom regarded as much worse than an excess of zeal.

At such times the neutral belt of ground separating Rivera from Santa Ana becomes a happy hunting-ground for both parties, where "pot-shots" at individuals escaping from either side to the other are held to be legitimate sport.

The disadvantages of such a condition of affairs were very clearly impressed upon my mind by the remarks of a resident photographer on the subject. Being asked why he kept the shutters up on his shop windows, as we could not see his wares to advantage inside the house, and had to take them out into the street to inspect them: "Well, you see," he replied, "no one can tell when they may begin to shoot, and the bullets destroy so many photographs, and break the 'negatives' if the

shutters are off, that I think it better to keep them up." It was impossible not to see the force of his reasoning, and one could not help sympathising with the artist. There was nothing querulous about his remark; he seemed to accept the ruling condition of affairs as natural, and no complaint escaped his lips as to the danger to himself or the members of his family from the action of the "patriots" and their opponents. His plaintive remarks applied solely to the damage to his stock in trade.

I had an opportunity of judging of other effects of a successful revolution which took place in Brazil while we were engaged upon the construction of the railway to Rivera. I was standing in a Brazilian hotel upon the frontier one night talking to the proprietor, when a policeman of the new régime came in. He was in plain clothes, the only indication of his calling being a rosette in his hat. He walked up to the bar and drank off some refreshment; then, turning towards the door, he made a sign to a party of his companions waiting there, who at once joined him, and all had drinks, which the policeman ordered. I noticed that when leaving he merely nodded to the bar-keeper, but made no payment. I asked the hotel owner if he allowed people to run up accounts on credit in such an indiscriminate manner, and he replied, " We have to give the new policemen and their friends drinks for nothing, otherwise they might revenge themselves upon us in some way."

That same revolution provided us with many object-lessons, of which I will only mention one other.

The Brazilian doctor who attended the engineer with the wounded leg had to fly the country. He had made the political mistake of favouring the losing side, which set many of his fellow-countrymen athirst to take his life. Fortunately he managed to escape in the darkness of the night-time, and arrived at one of our encampments, where he found shelter. From thence he got to the railway, by which he reached Montevideo, and embarked upon a steamer bound for Europe, there to await the return of more peaceful times in Brazil.

CHAPTER XX

IN REVOLUTIONARY TIMES

HAVING in the preceding chapter alluded to some of the discomforts that dwellers on the frontiers suffer during periods of political disturbance, it may be well before leaving the subject to consider other phases of it as applying to a more extended area.

It is curious how prevalent revolutions are in South America: they seem to spring up in the most unlikely places, when least expected, like those spiral columns of the air in motion which one frequently observes moving about upon the plains there, when all around them the atmosphere is absolutely still. Like them, too, some of the political disturbances do little more than stir up an immense amount of dust, while others overturn everything and create general confusion everywhere within the circular limits of their sphere of action, desolation marking their onward course.

It is many years since first I had an opportunity of witnessing a revolution in operation. I had but recently landed in South America, and was new to its peculiar ways, when a gentleman came to me one morning, in the office where I was at work, and told me that if I wished to see a revolution going on I could do so by merely looking out of one of the front windows of the house. I had heard the noise of what I took to be rockets going off, but paid no attention to it, knowing that the people enjoyed fireworks by daylight, and I thought they were amusing themselves with some harmless display of the kind.

I followed my friend's suggestion, and there I saw men fighting in the public street. It was my first experience of a revolution, and it proved to be only a trivial affair, more formidable looking than sanguinary, involving no very great loss of life after all, and it was soon ended.

Since then I have seen other similar political movements of various degrees of importance, but in one respect, they all seemed to me to bear a wonderful family likeness to each other. In each the patriots appeared to be burning with a pure and holy zeal to turn the Government of the day out of office for their misdeeds. But when the revolution was successful, and its leaders assumed the reins of power, they generally forgot those necessary reforms for which they had fought so manfully, and followed a very similar course to that they had so strongly denounced when pursued by their predecessors in office. Generally speaking, the only difference that is perceptible to lookers on at this game of political "beggar my neighbour," lies in the fact that the recipients of Government favours are different persons from those who previously enjoyed advantages of the kind.

It is a somewhat illogical proceeding, but no one seems to think it very irregular, and these movements have the advantage of furnishing the newspapers with a perennial subject for discussion, so long as they don't disapprove too strongly of the measures adopted by the Government for dealing with their opponents. If they venture upon adverse criticism it must be of the mildest type, otherwise the papers in which it appears are sure to be suppressed as dangerous to the safety of the State.

When matters arrive at this pass all further

speculation as to the progress of events is useless; there is nothing for it but to await patiently the development of affairs. One can, of course, follow the information given in the journals that have not been suppressed; but as this is invariably a version prepared and put forward by the party in power, its purport can usually be foretold without the trouble of wading through a "communicated" report, that deceives no one, for no one trusts it.

Strange things often take place in connection with insurrectionary movements in South America.

A friend of mine who had long been resident in that country was asked on one occasion by a general, just as if he was inviting him to a picnic, to accompany him and his staff the following day, in order to be present at a battle which was about to be fought with a party of insurgents. My friend not unnaturally asked to be excused, on the plea that he was not a soldier, and had no particular desire to witness scenes of bloodshed. At this the general laughed, and explained that there would be nothing of the kind, as the whole matter had been pre-arranged with the leader of

P

the rebels, who would submit after some firing of blank cartridge.

Next morning the Government troops marched forward, and opened a brisk fire upon the enemy from a great distance, giving them several tremendous volleys, whereupon the patriots prudently retired beyond the crest of the hill upon which they were posted.

Their leader then addressed them, explaining that he had been watching through his glass the effects of the firing of the soldiers, and that it was terrific. Fortunately they had not as yet got the right range, but when this was accurately ascertained, he feared it would soon be all up with his poor followers, facing such a diabolical weapon as the new "repeater." He could not bear the thought of his brave men, so badly armed as they were, being mowed down like grass, while unable to reply effectively at such a distance. He would risk his own life to save them, and would at once ride forward with a flag of truce to make the best terms that he could on their behalf with the enemy. If he was but successful in this respect, he cared not what happened to himself.

With these brave words upon his lips he rode

boldly forward towards the enemy, being accompanied by a volunteer, who held aloft a lance from which a white flag floated.

When they reached the lines of the Government troops they were met by an officer of the staff, who conducted the insurgent chief to the general's tent, where the two great men were left alone for half-an-hour. At the end of that time they both came forth, and ceremoniously saluting each other, the visitor rode away, escorted in like manner as upon his arrival.

It soon became known among the soldiers that the terms for the capitulation of the rebels had been arranged, while in the ranks of the latter there was much excitement and speculation about the result of the mission as they awaited the return of their chief.

When he arrived he explained that he had been entirely successful, even beyond his utmost hopes, so far as they were concerned. No punishment would be inflicted upon any of them, and they should be free to return at once to their respective homes as soon as they had laid down their arms and delivered them over to the soldiers. Moreover, all the reforms for which they had been fighting were to be conceded by the Government, and carried out.

These very favourable terms of capitulation he had only been able to secure for them by the sacrifice of his own interests, and by surrendering as a prisoner himself, unconditionally. He added that they needed not to grieve for him, for whatever might be his fate, his patriotic heart beat proudly in his bosom at the thought that, by his act of renunciation, he had gained for his companions-in-arms their lives and liberty. In the confusion of the moment he quite forgot to mention another item of gain that he had secured by the transaction, in the form of a substantial draft upon the Treasury of the Republic, which he had in his breast-pocket.

His audience seemed saddened for a moment by the personal misfortune and pathetic speech of their chief, but they had wonderfully elastic spirits. By the time they reached the soldiers, and had laid down their arms, they were quite cheerful again, and as friendly as possible with their enemies of an hour before, and willing to drink as many "treats" as they could get their conquerors to stand them.

It is said that in revolutionary times a good deal of such negotiating as I have been describing frequently goes on which is not made public, nor is good faith always kept between the parties to it.

An example of this kind occurred the last time I was out in South America, which made some little stir in the papers for a while, but it was soon forgotten.

It was an open secret to all who studied the signs of the times that revolutionary schemes were going on, though that, of course, was nothing very unusual. Prominent among the plotters was an ex-officer of the army; but the good faith of his adherence to the cause was doubted by another of the conspirators, who plainly told him so. "What!" said the angry soldier, "do you doubt my honour? but even if you do, can you not see that I have every reason in the world to be heart and soul with you in this matter?" With words like these he removed the doubts of all the men who were banded together, except those of him with whom they first arose. The latter stood aside, severing his connection with the movement; but matters went on in the revolutionary grooves, and the plot thickened.

The plan of action suggested by the ex-officer was that he, taking advantage of his acquaintance with his old colleagues in the army, should sound those in the chief garrison to see if they would be willing, and on what terms, to join the movement.

Negotiations with them went on satisfactorily, according to the reports of progress made from time to time. All was alleged to have been arranged for the troops in garrison to make common cause with the insurrectionary party when matters were ripe for doing so.

The occasion upon which the formal ratification of the compact was to take place was a banquet to be given by the military in their barracks. To this the leaders of the movement were invited, and when they had all assembled, they were surprised by the entrance of an armed body of soldiers, who proceeded at once to arrest the guests. The latter, when they found they had been betrayed, drew their revolvers, and defended themselves with desperation; but in the end, the survivors of them were overcome and secured, while several dead and dying men lay upon the bloodstained floor of the banqueting hall.

During this same attempt at revolution an official appeared in a country town, armed with full power from the Government to arrest all their opponents whom he thought it desirable to imprison. Of the authority so delegated to him he made a very free and full use during the absence of the principal Government official, who found the gaol full to overflowing upon his return home.

The special official requested permission to examine the prisoners, but this the chief refused. " I know what your interrogation means," he said, and he drew his hand suggestively across his throat. "Go back," he added, "and tell the Government they may dismiss me if they like; but so long as I hold the position I do, no man in the district under my charge shall suffer, except by the regular process of the law."

This ended the matter, the authorities being afraid to accept the challenge, and the imprisoned persons were released without further molestation.

During a revolution which occurred some years ago, a friend of mine was travelling in a railway train which was captured by insurgents. Some of the passengers being soldiers were put to death in presence of my friend, who had the good fortune to be let off when they discovered that he was an Englishman.

Another acquaintance of mine happened to be the manager of a large cattle farm, the owner of which was suspected of sympathising secretly with the party in revolt at the time. A large body of troops was sent out to quell the rising, and they encamped upon the property referred to. There they remained for a considerable time, killing the fattest cattle and the most highly bred, imported sheep for their daily food. When they moved on to other quarters, the manager politely asked the chief of the commissariat department to give him a written acknowledgment of the cattle and sheep they had taken for the troops, for future settlement.

But this officer explained that a document of the kind should be signed by the general in command, so the two men rode forward to see him about it.

When he heard the case stated, his reply to the manager was short and explicit, to this effect: "The only receipt I shall give you will be through the medium of a file of soldiers, at ten yards' distance, with loaded rifles. If you want that, you can have it at once."

I need scarcely add that the applicant did not wait for an acknowledgment of the kind, but mounted his horse without delay and rode off.

Another very unpleasant phase of the matter is, that during periods when the public peace is disturbed, or even threatened, by political movements, no rare occurrence, much power falls into the hands of irresponsible soldiers at times, and it is often used by them with cruel ingenuity to wreak their vengeance upon persons against whom they entertain some private cause of enmity. I have heard many harrowing tales from men who had been troopers, of crimes of the kind to which they have been eye-witnesses; but I will not repeat any of them, as they may have been exaggerated. I will mention a case bearing upon the same subject which a friend of mine heard from the principal actor in it. It struck me as exhibiting a curious way of looking at deeds of bloodshed, and a nice discrimination between methods of killing.

Revolutionary troubles were going on, and the narrator of the story was a soldier on the Government side. The fatigues of campaigning he bore with willingness, buoyed up by the hope that he would one day meet and square accounts with a deadly enemy of his whom he well knew took an active part upon the other side. Time rolled on, but his hoped-for chance seemed distant as ever, until one day, to his great delight, he recognised a straggler of the enemy, who was retreating after a skirmish, as the long-sought object of his hatred.

He gave immediate pursuit, and as he rode along he saw by the unsteady seat of the intended victim and the gait of his horse that both had been wounded in the fray. "I was delighted," he said, "for my horse was fresh, and there was a long stretch of marshy land before us, and I knew I should overtake my enemy when we got to it. I gained on him at every stride," he went on, "and he had scarcely got a hundred yards into the rough ground when his horse floundered through a soft place and fell. I was up with them in a moment, and there lay my enemy helplessly upon his back, too weak from the loss of blood to rise to his feet. I got my knee upon his chest, and grasped him by the hair in my left hand, while I drew my knife to cut his throat, but he looked up so pitifully at me, that I could not bear to do it."

Here my friend interrupted him, saying he had acted quite properly, as one should always spare an enemy when powerless and at his mercy.

"No, señor!" was the indignant reply; and when asked to explain what he had done, he continued, "I turned my face away and drove the knife into his heart."

On another occasion a man whom I knew was stopping at a small country inn when a party of soldiers arrived with a prisoner, both of whose hands had been cut off as a punishment for his having taken part in a revolution. The unfortunate captive in his agony begged to be put to death, and the officer in charge sanctioned his request, simply telling his men to take him outside and cut his throat.

The recent revolution in Uruguay, which was only brought to a close in the autumn of last year (1897), if indeed it is a real peace, not a temporary truce, that has been effected, offers many subjects for reflection that deserve careful consideration.

Perhaps no better example could be found of the utterly untrustworthy nature of the official statements published during such political upheavals. In relation to it we were repeatedly told, on the authority of the Government, and in the most circumstantial manner, that it was suppressed and at an end, after a decisive victory over the insurgents, who were nearly all slain and the survivors dispersed.

Yet these conquered and scattered remnants of a revolutionary party had the awkward knack of turning up again after each such suppression in stronger force than previously, and closer to the seat of government, till in the end the latter appeared to be at their mercy, and peace was made with them. It is only fair to add that, in the case of the revolution of which I am writing, its object seemed to have been, as well as one can judge of the matter from the published reports, to bring about much needed reforms, and to suppress abuses that were ruining the State.

During the disturbance referred to there was a tragic episode, the assassination of the President of the Republic, who was shot on the steps of the cathedral in Montevideo by a soldier. The foul deed was thought at first to have been inspired by political motives, but it proved to be due to private revenge.

This is but one example of the many evils arising from the revolutionary spirit which too frequently pervades society, deadening the moral perceptions of its members, and inculcating a disregard for law and order.

It is easy to understand how, from such conditions, a feverish and unwholesome state of existence should ensue, highly detrimental to the progress and prosperity of the country.

Its credit is injured in the foreign markets, and the difficulty of raising capital, so necessary for the development of its resources, is correspondingly increased. Immigration, which it should be the especial care of a prudent Government to foster by every legitimate means, is paralysed and discouraged. The insecurity of life and property that prevails during political commotions tends to deter those in search of a new country from settling there, and induces them to seek elsewhere more peaceful homes. The injury thus inflicted upon the country is incalculable

CHAPTER XXI

NATURAL HISTORY NOTES

DURING the whole of the time occupied by the construction of the railway I was far too busy to have much opportunity for shooting, or personally collecting information relating to sporting matters or the habits of beasts and birds. There are some brief references to the latter part of the subject in other chapters, which I shall now endeavour to supplement by a few further observations on kindred matters.

It has already been mentioned that the larger and more dangerous wild animals are fast disappearing from Uruguay before the increase of flocks and herds, but wild-cats and foxes are still much more numerous there than the inhabitants of the country like. An enormous specimen of the former was shot in the valley of the Tambores by one of the workmen on the railway. I had seen many others, both alive and dead, but none before approaching that one in size, or of such formidable appearance.

Deer of the species *Cervus campestris* are frequently to be met with in the open country, as already mentioned in these pages, but the larger deer, with more massive antlers, which keep to the woods or their immediate vicinity, are being rapidly exterminated.

I met with but one specimen of them alive, among thick brushwood in a river valley, though I have frequently seen their skins exposed for sale in shops.

Armadilloes of various kinds are very common, and one occasionally meets with the great anteater.

Upon the bank of the river Tres Cruces I saw a beautiful black marten, about the size of a domestic cat, but shaped like a stoat.

It is somewhat remarkable that biscachoes, which are so common in Buenos Ayres, are not to be found in Uruguay.

Carpinchoes, or water-hogs, are numerous, as are also nutrias, an animal like a huge water-rat, the size of a cat.

In the little river Guayavos I once saw an

ordinary otter, under circumstances that could not admit of my being mistaken about its identity. In the Rio Negro, as also in the Tacuarembó Grande, I repeatedly saw huge fresh-water seals. I have heard it stated by people living near these rivers that such animals will attack a dog in the water and drown him.

As to birds, I must naturally give first place to eagles, of which there are three different kinds to be met with in Uruguay, distinguished by the colours black, brown, and blue. The last mentioned is the largest of them, the other two being about equal in size, and all three considerably smaller than their European relations.

When seen in the sunlight at a particular angle the brown eagle appears to be golden-coloured. Both it and the blue species fly rather heavily, but the flight of the black eagle is perfect in every respect. Nothing can be more easy and graceful than it is. They rise high into the air or skim along the surface of the ground with equal ease and motionless wings, whether with or against the wind.

They are very destructive to partridge. Two dead birds of the kind were found in a nest from which we took a young eagle, almost fully grown, but yet unable to fly. That they occasionally vary the nature of their food I had an opportunity of learning when hidden one day in the thick woods of the Tambores valley. My attention was attracted by the noisy contentions of birds of prey in my immediate neighbourhood, that seemed to be disputing for the possession of some choice dainty they had discovered. After a while the turbulent assembly broke up and flew away.

In their flight they passed close to where I lay concealed, and I was able to ascertain the cause of all their quarrelling. An eagle, with a writhing snake in its talons, led the procession, followed closely by a number of very angry hawks, that loudly demanded to share the spoil; while some hungry vultures, at a more respectful distance, openly proclaimed their disapprobation of the whole affair.

A curious flock of birds of prey, like falcons, were frequently to be seen in the valley of the Tacuarembó Chico, hunting together on the wing, to the number of twelve or fourteen, just as a pack of beagles would do on the ground.

Turning now to game-birds, the best of these

in Uruguay is the bronze-coloured pheasant, locally known as the Pavo del Monte, or wood-turkey. It is somewhat larger than an ordinary pheasant, and the prevailing colour of the plumage is a dark-bronzed green, almost approaching black. On the neck, breast, and shoulder the feathers are slightly tipped with white, as are also some of the covering feathers of the wing at its point. The back of the bird from the shoulder down is of a dark brownish-green. The throat and sides of the neck adjoining it are bare for a length of nearly two inches, and of a red colour. The first two of the primary feathers in each wing are very curiously formed. Number one has only the same narrow width of feathering, for two inches from the point, on the concave side of the central quill rib that it has on its convex side, and then it widens out like the feathers of an ordinary bird to three or four times that width. In the case of the second primary feather the same peculiarity exists, but only for a length of one inch and a half; while the third and succeeding feathers are of the ordinary shape all the way from the point. The extreme length of the bird from the bill to the end of the tail is two feet six inches. The tail itself, in which there are eleven feathers, is eleven and a half inches long, and it is broad at the end, not pointed like that of an ordinary pheasant. Lastly the length of the leg is ten inches.

The Pavo del Monte flies well and strongly, but it is unwilling to take to the wing, and keeps much to the thick foliage among the top branches of high trees. Its call or cry is somewhat like that of a turkey, to which the name it has received in Spanish is probably due, as in most other respects it is very unlike a turkey. In Uruguay it is held in much esteem as a table delicacy. I cannot say that my own taste corroborates this opinion, as those which I shot I found to be rather coarse in flavour, but this may perhaps have been caused by the cooking of them.

I heard a curious tale of a Pavo del Monte shooting a man, which was positively asserted to be true. The bird in question had been wounded, but only winged, and ran away when it fell to the ground. The man who fired at it laid down his gun hurriedly and gave chase, when a game of "hide and seek" took place among the brushwood. In one of its doublings and turnings the pavo passed over the gun, which was lying on the ground, and its toes happened to strike against the trigger of the undischarged barrel, the hammer of which in the hurry of the moment had been left at full cock, with the result that the charge went off and wounded the sportsman.

Birds, we know, are sometimes taught to fire off pistols in those exhibitions known as " Happy Families," as well as to perform other unusual feats; but it is not often that a wild bird in the woods shoots a man with his own gun, as this one did in Uruguay.

Partridges of two kinds, small and large (*Nothura maculosa* and *Rhyncotus rufescens*), were formerly very plentiful in Uruguay, but they are becoming scarcer year by year. Eagles and sportsmen with firearms are not their only enemies. The natives of the country are very expert in snaring them. A boy of ours who was employed looking after the horses while grazing, was very smart at taking partridges by means of a loop made with an ostrich feather attached to the end of a long bamboo cane.

I saw another boy catching the smaller partridge in a most ingenious way. He rode along until he saw a partridge, and then dismounting, set about his plan of attack. The surface of the ground was rough at the place where I watched him at work, and he selected an opening five or six inches wide, between two rocks, in which he laid a wire snare, just as if he were setting it for a rabbit. This done, he proceeded to look up the partridge, which had been hiding during the operation, and having disturbed it once more, drove it gradually, in the most skilful manner, into his trap, and then walked up and took his fluttering prize.

Of course this plan would only suit with birds that are great runners, and unwilling to take to the wing.

In winter one meets with many wild duck of different kinds, though they are not nearly as numerous as in the Argentine province of Buenos Ayres. This latter remark will also apply to snipe, which I had the curious experience of shooting over a bull-terrier, that was exceedingly well trained to point them.

While in Uruguay I saw another example of misdirected energies, in the case of a sporting pig. It had been reared along with some dogs, and became very much attached to them. At a later period, when they were brought out to search for game, the pig always accompanied its canine friends and ranged about with them. Whenever it met with an obstacle in its path that it could not leap over, its cries at being left behind were piteous to hear. The dogs, its companions, would frequently on such occasions return to assist and encourage it to renewed exertions to scramble over the difficulty.

I missed this curious pointer on one of my visits to the district, and from the laughing reply that I got to my inquiries about it, I fear poor piggie, notwithstanding its unusual sporting propensities, had gone the way that so many others of its race had travelled before it.

I once met with a giant stork that was a perfect grenadier beside its companions of the ordinary kind. These latter were common enough, and I have seen them in great flocks flying high up in the air during their periodical migrations.

One that was made a pet of by the engineers at a hut upon the works became very tame, and was a great favourite, performing a number of tricks when told to do so, and remained with them all the year round.

There was a bird closely allied to the storks of which I made the acquaintance in Uruguay. Taking advantage of the cover afforded by a thick growth of shrubs and brushwood, I managed to get close to it, and was able to observe its movements carefully through a field-glass, without being seen myself. When in search of food it walked into the water where there was a current, and instead of striking at its prey, as the storks and herons do, it placed its bill in the water in such a position as it would occupy if the bird was engaged in examining its own legs. The mandibles were kept apart in an inverted position. By this means the water flowed between them, and from time to time they were brought together and closed with a snap upon some small fish or insect that was passing through. If what had been seized proved upon reflection to be edible, the bird raised its head and swallowed the morsel, and then resumed its former attitude; but if the object seemed uninviting, the mandibles were merely opened again, and the prisoner was allowed to escape. As I subsequently obtained one of these birds, I am enabled to give a more accurate description of it.

The body is white; but the primary and secondary wing feathers are of a beautiful dark green, with metallic lustre, resembling the tail feathers of a magpie. There are twelve similar green feathers in the tail, the last one on each side having a tendency to white on its inside or covered edge.

The neck is rather shorter, in proportion to the size of the body, than that of an ordinary stork, and it is of a brownish colour. The forehead is quite bald, and the upper part of the bill, which is yellow, is very coarse and large where it is set on to the head; but it tapers much towards the point, where it is slightly curved and rounded, being intended for the purpose of preventing food escaping from the bill, not for striking at it. The legs are slate-coloured, and are bare to a height of 5 inches above the joint, to allow for deep wading. The eyes are dark-coloured. This bird when standing in a natural and erect position is about 31 inches high. The length of the body is 9 inches, that of the neck 8 inches, that of the bill $7\frac{1}{2}$ inches. The upper joint of the leg is 10 inches, and the lower one 7 inches.

Here I may also give some particulars of a bird to which reference has been already made more than once in these pages, and which, for want of a better name, I have called the brown stork.

In some respects it differs considerably from the storks, much more closely resembling the ibis family in appearance. It lacks, however, the regular curved bill common to the latter, as the one it possesses is straight almost down to the end, where it is only slightly curved.

The ordinary height of the bird when standing in a natural position is about 2 feet. Its extreme length stretched out is 3 feet $1\frac{1}{2}$ inch. The length of leg is 14 inches; the toes are very long, the central one being $4\frac{1}{2}$ inches. The bill is $4\frac{5}{8}$ inches, the lower mandible ending in a very fine point, which fits into a hollow in the upper one prepared to receive it.

The colour of the bird appears to be black when seen at a distance, but when examined closely it is a dark olive-brown. The primary wing-feathers are almost black. There are small white markings on the feathers of the back of the neck, from the head down to the shoulders, and on the angles of the wings. The eyes are brown, and the legs slate-coloured.

Its dreadful cry was referred to elsewhere.

While in Uruguay I had an aviary, in which I kept a number of birds that various people sent me. Among them were a pair of beautiful buff egrets, a large partridge, and many small birds of various kinds, all of which lived on friendly terms together, with the exception of one Cardinal bird, that displayed the most ill-bred manners I ever saw in any member of the feathered tribe. Its constant habit was to hop up to other birds, especially if new arrivals, and look them full in the face, first with its head on one side then on the other, and finally toss it up in the air as if implying, "I don't think much of you." One bird only in the whole collection knew how to deal properly with this pert Cardinal. It was of small size, but possessed a sharp bill and a wonderfully capacious throat, which it opened wide whenever the Cardinal approached it. This form of reception gradually taught the objectionable intruder better manners. Among the collection there were Calandrias, the best singing birds of South America, and other specimens, some with showy plumage, others clothed in sombre colours.

An interesting and pleasing incident connected with my aviary was the escape and return of one of its inmates. A bird got out and flew away so far, that it was lost to sight in the distance. This occurred in the morning, and the same evening, towards nightfall, the truant came back, and alighted upon the roof of the aviary, waiting to be let in again. When the door was opened it flew down to the ground and walked in as if it had only been out for the day on leave.

Then there were the uncaged and casual pets which we had from time to time. Among them may be mentioned an eagle, and two owls of different kinds, and the most charming of all, a young ostrich, which was captured and taken with us when making the surveys for the line of railway. In a couple of days it became quite tame, and never attempted to escape. Towards nightfall it would come and ask, in the most doleful little whistle, to be put to bed, where it was quite happy. In the mornings it always accompanied the men when they went to catch the horses, in which operation it seemed to take great delight. Wherever the confusion was greatest there it was always to be found rushing wildly in and out among the men and horses, and getting into every person's way. It was irresistibly comical, and reminded one of the officious clown at the circus, who persists in appearing to help every one else, while in reality he is giving them no assistance whatever, but rather retarding their operations.

Besides the birds I had other pets; among them should be mentioned a coati (*Nasua narica*). It was a native of Brazil, somewhat larger than a raccoon, an animal to which it bore some resemblance in general appearance; but it possessed a much larger head, with a longer and more pig-like snout. It was very tame and harmless.

Another creature I possessed was a large tortoise, about which there was nothing very remarkable except the late hours it kept. During the daytime it seemed to sleep quietly at home in a barrel of water, but when darkness set in it used to climb out of the barrel and descend by the primitive method of dropping on to the ground on its back, the shell of which protected the body from injury from the concussion of the fall, and then it went off to visit its friends or examine the locality.

What to do with my pets when the time should come round for me to leave South America often occasioned me some anxious thoughts. The tortoise settled the matter as far as it was concerned, by going off on its own account. The two owls followed its example. The coati I gave back to the person from whom I originally got it. Another kind friend took the whole of the inmates of the aviary, and would no doubt tend them with even more care than I bestowed on them myself.

While residing at San Fructuoso I became acquainted with an old French sportsman, who made his living by fishing and shooting.

He was one of Nature's gentlemen, whom it is a pleasure to meet. When a young man he had been a cavalry soldier in France, and on one occasion a vicious horse caught him up in his teeth, and shook him as a dog would a rat, fearfully injuring the bone of his left arm. The army surgeon was for immediate amputation, but the man begged so hard against the operation that the surgeon desisted, and left him to his own devices. His comrades bandaged up the injured limb in their own rough way, and in time it healed; but their job was not a neat one from a professional point of view, as the setting of the bone was very crooked. It was better to have a crooked arm, however, than none at all, as he was able to make considerable, though awkward, use of it. He used to bring me fish and game in their respective seasons, and I often got rare specimens of birds from him, which I was glad to add to my collection. He was also able occasionally to supply information regarding them that I could not otherwise have obtained.

CHAPTER XXII

CLIMATE OF URUGUAY

ALTHOUGH Uruguay is very hot in summer, the climate of the country is good and healthy. Mr. M. G. Mulhall, in his excellent "Handbook of the River Plate," gives the highest temperature at Montevideo for the years 1884, 1885, and 1886 as 101°, 96°, and 100° Fahrenheit in the shade, and the lowest reading of the thermometer for the same years, in the same place, as 35°, 34°, and 35° Fahrenheit respectively.

During the years 1890 and 1891 I kept a careful register of the temperature at the Paso de los Toros, which was about 2° 20′ north of Montevideo. As might be expected, it was perceptibly warmer there in summer, being so much closer to the tropics; but on the other hand, it was considerably colder in winter. This no doubt was due to the proximity to the sea at Montevideo, which would have a moderating influence upon the cold as well as upon the heat.

Summer may be assumed to last from the beginning of November till the end of February. Of the 120 days comprised within these four summer months, we found that two-thirds of them had a maximum temperature of 80° Fahrenheit and upwards in the shade, made up thus:—

    30 days, with a maximum temperature of 80°– 90°
    34   ,,   ,,   ,,   90°–100°
    16   ,,   ,,   ,,   100°–110°

Total 80 days, with a temperature from 80° to 110° Fahrenheit in the shade.

Whenever three or four excessively warm days came together they were generally followed by a very cool one.

As regards the coldest night in winter for the three years that Mr. Mulhall deals with, 3°, 2°, and 3° Fahrenheit above freezing-point were, as already stated, the lowest temperatures registered, whereas we frequently had it much lower, and more than once it touched 24° Fahrenheit with us, or 8° of frost. Ice was frequently to be seen on the water in the side ditches of the railway.

Comparing the annual rainfall for the same period, Mr. Mulhall gives it as 38, 37, and 36 inches respectively. We found these figures to correspond approximately with our observations for the year 1890; but it was worthy of remark that on the 6th March of that year 6.30 inches fell, or one-sixth of total.

1891 was unusually wet, it having rained on ninety days of that season, making up a total rainfall of 60 inches, or nearly double the average one.

The two heaviest days' rain during that period were respectively six inches and 5.70 inches in the twenty-four hours. These figures, however, afford no adequate idea of how heavy the rain is at times. On one occasion half an inch fell in five minutes, on another eight-tenths of an inch in fifteen minutes, and one inch in half-an-hour. Twice the rainfall was between four-tenths and half an inch in twenty minutes; one and one-tenth inch fell in an hour, and two inches fell in two hours. These facts suggest how tropical the rain can be in Uruguay at times.

For a month before the regular summer season begins and for a like period after it ends, that is, for the months of October and March, the weather is generally delightful. Throughout the winter too there are frequently many very fine days.

During dry, hot summers dust storms are very prevalent. At the approach of a visitation of the kind, though the sun may have been shining brightly in the sky at noonday, its light is soon obscured by the dust clouds as they advance, until an almost Egyptian darkness prevails. The atmosphere becomes most suffocating, and one finds difficulty in breathing it in consequence of the quantity of impalpable dust floating suspended in it.

I have had many unpleasant experiences of travelling under such circumstances, one of which presented a rather unusual incident.

I was riding accompanied by one of our men, when a storm of the kind burst upon us. So great was the difficulty of breathing, that I took out my pocket-handkerchief and held it over my mouth to act as a respirator, and intercept some of the dust with which the air was laden. While proceeding in this manner at a walking pace along the road a sudden gust of wind blew the handkerchief away, and my companion jumped off his horse and ran after it into the darkness.

He soon returned and handed me what we both took to be my lost property which he had recovered, but on examination it proved to be a totally different pocket-handkerchief that he brought back. Of course the ready explanation that will occur to the reader is, that I had been making use of a pocket-handkerchief that was not my own, which had been sent back to me from the wash by mistake, and only discovered the fact upon its loss and recovery, as described above. But this could not have been the case, for the handkerchief blown out of my hand had a mourning border on it, which the one returned to me had not.

The suggestion I would make is, that a similar mishap occurred in the case of some other traveller who had passed along the road before us, and that he had failed to recover his handkerchief, which the man riding with me found when looking for mine.

Such storms as I have been describing are nearly always followed by heavy rain, which lays the dust and clears the air. This is generally accompanied by thunderstorms, which are very frequent and severe in Uruguay during the summer. I remember one of them that lasted for nearly twelve hours with scarcely any intermission. On two occasions a house quite close to me was struck by lightning and damaged, but in neither case were the inmates injured. Men, houses, cattle and sheep are frequently struck by lightning and killed.

Sometimes very heavy hailstones fall during or immediately after a thunderstorm, doing great damage to crops and sheep. One such hailstone that we measured was $3\frac{1}{8}$ inches long by two inches broad and two inches thick, or larger than a goose egg, and there were several others lying on the ground that did not seem much smaller.

There are summer visitors which occasionally arrive in these countries that are not always welcomed. I allude to the flights of locusts, which come in clouds so thick, that neither spurs nor whip will force a horse to face them at times; and when they alight, they stay until they have eaten up every green thing that is within their reach and capable of consumption.

The poor people whose gardens they attack rush out beating tin pans, kettles, and fire-irons, somewhat like the practice in the case of swarming bees at home, only the object is different in the two cases, the intention being to attract the bees, but to drive off the locusts.

American stories about railway trains having been stopped by a flight of locusts appear to some people to be gross exaggerations, but they are the simple truth. When locusts alight upon the rails in such great numbers that their crushed bodies yield a lubricating substance causing the wheels of the engine to slip, its power of traction is lost, with the natural result that the train is brought to a stand-still upon the first incline it meets where the locusts are in force.

There are few things more difficult of accomplishment than to keep one's self cool and comfortable during intensely hot weather. That hero of our school-days, Achilles, was, we know, vulnerable only in the heel, but it is at the other end, the head, that ordinary mortals are most liable to suffer injury from excessive heat. Under such circumstances it is not surprising that various attempts should have been made from time to time in different lands to provide an artificial protection for this sensitive extremity.

Turbans, pith-helmets, air-chambered hats, and a pugaree have their respective advocates, and no doubt much could be said in favour of each of them; but by far the most extraordinary means for keeping one's head cool in hot weather was a plan adopted by a young office-boy, of Irish nationality, that we had in Uruguay. It had, however, two serious defects, which would, no doubt, militate against its general adoption. One of these was, that it was not of a portable nature, so that it could not be worn while walking about; the other was, that it interfered considerably with the sense of hearing of the person protected by it.

I discovered the boy's invention in this way. The weather was very hot, and I called out, "Tom, bring me a glass of water from the refrigerator," but received no reply. I then raised my voice and called him, repeating the operation several times, but with a like ineffectual result. So I thought I should go and fetch the water myself, as Tom had apparently given himself leave of absence and gone off duty. Upon reaching the refrigerator I found the missing Tom with his head down in it, and discovered to my surprise that this was his usual way of cooling himself when his head began to "swell with the heat," as he expressed it.

It is perhaps unnecessary to add that I prescribed a change of treatment to effect his purpose for subsequent attacks of the kind.

Here I may make a few remarks about him, though they are not of a meteorological nature.

Tom was not a bad boy in his way, but he had peculiarities that he would have been better without. He was born and brought up near a large military station in Ireland, on the road between the barracks and the cemetery, and had acquired a great admiration for the "Dead March," which he used to hear played at soldiers' funerals.

Unfortunately he had a quick musical ear, and as he was never tired of whistling the melancholy dirge with variations of his own, introduced apparently for the purpose of imparting a more lively spirit to it, the result was most lugubrious.

Another failing of his was an innate persuasion that he could improve on all orders given him.

One evening he was told to lead a saddle-horse, which was not very easy to manage, from my hut to the stable-yard. Tom, however, thought riding preferable to walking, so he mounted, and proceeded in this manner until some difference of opinion arose between him and the horse. The latter, not approving of the turn affairs had taken, cantered off, increasing his pace to a gallop as he went along. When they reached the yard gate it was shut, which brought the horse to a standstill, but not so his rider, who was thrown over it. The unfortunate boy came back to me in a sad plight, denouncing the horse's viciousness, and proclaiming that all his own ribs and one of his arms were broken. It was not quite so bad as this, as he had only received a severe shaking, and was very sore all over from the fall.

Among the curious atmospheric phenomena that I observed on several occasions were meteorites shooting upwards like the discharge of rockets. They generally occurred in the south.

Once while walking along the railway, a couple of hours after nightfall, the moon being well up in the sky, not far from full, and shining brightly at the time, my attention was suddenly attracted by the appearance of a magnificent meteor in the north, which travelled slowly eastwards towards the moon in an almost horizontal course for some seconds and then disappeared. It seemed to be about one-fourth of the size of the moon.

CHAPTER XXIII

RAILWAYS OF URUGUAY

At the present day it will scarcely be disputed that facilities for travelling and for the transport of goods are essential to the progress and prosperity of a nation.

It is in the ability to deliver articles of barter at a market where their sale can be effected that lies their practical value. The gem or mineral at the mine, if irremovable, has no realisable worth beyond that possessed by the coarser rock surrounding it; and the excess of farm produce over that which can be consumed upon the spot is similarly valueless under like conditions.

I have seen many acres of fine wheat, ripe for the sickle, set fire to and burnt, in order to get clear of it, the cost of transporting it to market being greater than the price it would fetch there.

Bearing these principles in mind, and applying them to the case of Uruguay, we find in it an example of a country pre-eminently depending for the development of its resources, and the consequent prosperity of its people, upon the facilities afforded for the transport of its produce and articles of consumption.

Of public roads worthy of the name there are none throughout the length and breadth of the land, except—and such exceptions are rare—in the vicinity of towns.

The means of communication in times gone by were merely rights of way across the various properties that intervened between the traveller and his destination, and when the track became impassable from rain and traffic, one had only to go to either side of it in search of better ground on which to continue his journey. Lately, however, these circumstances have altered greatly.

Wire fencing has been introduced and largely adopted in the country. So-called roads, which, more correctly speaking, are mere sites or allowances for roads, have been fenced off and separated from the adjoining properties, so that traffic is concentrated within narrower limits than formerly, with the result that the hollows where rain collects become so worked into mud, as frequently to be impassable for wheels in wet weather. This makes the conveyance of produce or merchandise by bullock carts, which are the ordinary means of transport of the country, both tedious and costly, not to mention the chance of injury to the goods from exposure to the weather on the journey.

These conditions tend to break down competition from such a source, and to demonstrate more clearly the advantages of carriage by rail.

It was not until the year 1867 that the *vis inertiæ* of public opinion in Uruguay upon the subject of the necessity for improved means of communication between the capital and the interior was finally overcome. In that year a railway was begun near Montevideo by a local company, with the intention of pushing it northwards to the central town of Durazno, a distance of $127\frac{1}{2}$ miles. The project was, however, far too great for the means available for its execution, and only 6 miles of the line were then constructed.

In the year 1871 the enterprise was taken seriously in hand by a new company that had been formed in London, and the section to Santa Lucia, 37 miles from Montevideo, was opened the following year.

In 1874 it was extended for another 90½ miles to Durazno, a portion of this length having been previously opened for traffic. The following year a branch of 20 miles was completed from about the fortieth mile on the main line to the town of San José, being a part of what was then called the Central Uruguay and Higueritas Railway.

In this condition matters remained till 1880, when a couple of miles, from Durazno to the north side of the river Yi, were added to the main line.

In 1886 an extension of 38 miles, to a little south of the Rio Negro, was opened, and the large and important bridge across that river was finished in January 1887, making the total length of the line then brought into traffic 190 miles.

This constitutes the whole of the original Central Uruguay line; but as the system now comprises other undertakings, it may be well to give the details of the latter here. The first of these was a line of some twenty miles in length, extending from Montevideo, in an eastwardly direction, to the small town of Pando, that gave its name to the undertaking which was then known as the Pando Railway. Its infancy was not of a robust character; in fact, it was quite the reverse, and it was re-christened more than once, apparently with the hope of obtaining for it some benefit by the process.

The modesty of its original designation having failed to attract the attention it merited, it was changed to the alliterative and more pretentious title of the Montevideo, Minas, and Maldonado Railway, but without any perceptible increase of luck.

It had struggled from 1875 till 1880 for a feeble existence, and various concessions, or modifications of concessions, were then and subsequently obtained for the purpose of strengthening its constitution. But it was not till 1888 that it was strong enough to stand alone; and it was opened in that year, from Montevideo to Minas, 76 miles, under the name of the North-Eastern of Uruguay Railway.

Its success was at once assured, as it was seen that the district it served could yield a fair traffic; but it did not long retain its separate and independent character, for in 1889 it was leased and taken over by the Central Uruguay

Railway Company. Out of this grew another branch, or more correctly, a completely new "shoot," as it was a distinct and separate, although allied, undertaking—the Central Uruguay Eastern Extension Railway—from Toledo Station, on the North-Eastern line, to Nico-Perez, a length of 128 miles, part of which was opened in 1890 and the remainder in 1891.

In the preceding year a junction line 5 miles long was made near Montevideo, to connect the eastern section more perfectly with the Central Railway by which it was leased.

In the year 1888 another friendly project had been set on foot, under the title of the Central Uruguay Northern Extension Railway, to continue the main line northwards from the Rio Negro to the Brazilian frontier, a distance which proved to be $182\frac{1}{4}$ miles. It was for the construction of this railway that the writer went out to South America for the third time, and remained there more than three years. The works were begun in 1889, 41 miles were opened in 1890, 68 more in 1891, and the remaining $73\frac{1}{4}$ miles in 1892.

From the foregoing it will be seen that the Central Uruguay Railway system consists of a main or trunk line of 352¼ miles from Montevideo to the Brazilian frontier at Rivera, with branches or allied lines to the extent of 229 miles, making a total of 581¼ miles.

It also draws traffic from lines that form junctions with its systems, but with the management of which it has no concern.

One of these is styled the Uruguay Great Eastern Railway, of which, however, only 31 miles, that were made five or six years ago, are as yet in traffic. It branches off from the North-Eastern Railway at Olmos Junction, close to Pando, and extends to La Sierra, in the direction of Maldonado.

Another and much more important line of this description is the Midland Railway. It has a junction with the Central Uruguay at Rio Negro, 170 miles north of Montevideo, and is 196½ miles long, rather more than half of the distance being the section between Rio Negro and Paysandu, on the river Uruguay, which town lies in the direction of north-west by west from Rio Negro. The second section runs northwards, approximately parallel to the course of the Uruguay, as far as the town of Salto, where it joins the North-Western Railway. It was constructed some nine years ago.

The North-Western Railway, to which allusion has just been made, was begun and partly finished more than twenty years ago. It extends from Salto, for 111 miles, in a northerly direction to the Brazilian frontier at Santa Rosa.

At a station called Isla de Cabellos, on the North-Western Railway, 72 miles north of Salto, a line called the Northern Railway branches off in a north-eastwardly direction for San Eugenio, on the Brazilian frontier, a distance of 70 miles.

There was a projected line, called the Uruguay Western Railway. The scheme contemplated the making of a line from Montevideo to Colonia, on the Rio de la Plata. Part of the idea was to purchase and utilise the line of rails $14\frac{1}{4}$ miles long, from Montevideo to the slaughter yards for cattle, as a means of getting into the city.

The affair collapsed at the time, but several attempts have since been made to resuscitate it.

Such being the actual state of the railways of Uruguay, to judiciously extend the existing system by the construction of the necessary branch lines to reach the various districts, according as the increase of population and the progress of the country require them, should be the true progressive policy to follow.

It is to be hoped that the lesson taught by the railway mania of eight or nine years ago in the Argentine Republic will long be remembered in Uruguay.

During that craze, in a few months, new lines were proposed in Argentina to the extent of twenty-three thousand miles, or more than four times the total length then open for traffic—the growth of the previous thirty years. In the case of some of these projects, the promoters made no stipulation as to receiving any financial assistance; but the majority of applicants for concessions asked the government to guarantee the payment of a fixed rate of interest upon capital to the immense aggregate amount of about sixty-six millions sterling, for projects that were, for the most part, absolutely worthless.

To those who knew the country and its resources, it was evident that such so-called progress was not due to increased strength in the beat of life-blood in the national pulse, but to a fevered temperature produced by a mania, having its outcome in the scramble for railway concessions.

Injudicious railway expenditure of the kind tends only to embarrass the country by adding to its indebtedness, without in any way assisting to develop its resources. Nor does the evil stop there; for worthless undertakings cast discredit upon others that are sound and good enough, and thus retard the carrying out of works that might be of great public utility and value.

The following tabular statement will serve to show at a glance the growth of railways in Uruguay, as well as their present position :—

URUGUAYAN RAILWAYS

TABULAR STATEMENT SHOWING THEIR PROGRESS AND EXTENT *

Name of Railway.	Gauge of Line.	Length of Railways open for Traffic at close of Years					
		1870.	1875.	1880.	1885.	1890.	1895.
	Ft. In.	Miles.	Miles.	Miles.	Miles.	Miles.	Miles.
Central Uruguay Railway							
Main Line (Montevideo to Rio Negro)	4 8½	6	127½	130	130	170	170
Branch to San José	,,	...	20	20	20	20	20
Eastern Extension	,,	...	...	...	...	35½	128
North-Eastern of Uruguay	,,	...	...	20	20	76	76
Northern Extension	,,	...	...	...	...	40¾	182¼
Peñarol Junction	,,	...	...	...	...	5	5
Total Central System		6	147½	170	170	347¼	581¼
Uruguay Great Eastern Railway	,,	...	...	...	...	...	31
Midland Uruguay Railway	,,	...	...	...	...	196½	196½
North-Western of Uruguay	,,	...	45	63	72	111	111
Uruguay Northern	,,	...	...	...	...	33½	70
,, Western	,,	...	...	...	...	14¾	14¾
Total		6	192½	233	242	702¾	1004

* There has been no increase in the length of the railways open to traffic since 1895.

CHAPTER XXIV

CONCLUSION

PERHAPS it may be thought that in the preceding pages I have assumed too much of the rôle of "candid friend," exposing so many skeletons in South American cupboards.

Why, it may be asked, drag them into the light of publicity? Why write of the little failings of military men, of lawyers, and others in various callings? Why draw dismal pictures of the insecurity of life, of revolutionary times, and of the mean developments of political intrigues? Why not ignore such unpleasant subjects altogether, and foster the belief that they have no existence, save in the imaginative brains of journalists in need of sensational "copy"?

To such suggestions my reply would be that you may wrap the *poncho* of pretended ignorance around the bony shoulders of the skeletons, and strive by that means to hide their hideous deformity; but they will continue to look down upon you, and meet the public gaze with ghastly and familiar leers, as clearly as they would under the prying search of the "Röntgen rays."

Ignoring the facts will not cure the disease. It is but postponing the evil day when it must be dealt with; for if the country is to advance with the times, the skeletons must be ruthlessly laid bare and banished, never to return. They should be relegated without delay to the glass cases of the national museums as curious specimens from bygone days. Professors of political anatomy would there be able to examine them at their leisure, and draw from that source a wholesome warning wherewith to caution future generations.

Not one word that I have given expression to has been written in an unfriendly spirit. It is true that some of the incidents herein narrated may reflect upon "all sorts and conditions of men," but it must not be assumed that society generally approves of or is fairly represented by the more objectionable of them. On the contrary, their misdeeds are repudiated and condemned by the wholesome and robust portion of public opinion in the countries where they occur. The local press deals with them in scathing denunciations, couched in language compared with which the strongest of my remarks are mild to the verge of feebleness.

My firm conviction is, that the great wants of South American States are rest and freedom from political upheaval and disturbance, and a strict adherence not only to the letter, but also to the spirit of all their engagements; a state of things which peace would tend to foster.

Such a condition of affairs can only exist under just and strong governments, careful to make the laws respected, and to afford efficient protection to all who reside in or have dealings with the countries under their control. To accomplish these objects local politicians should devote all their best energies.

It would not seem to demand any great sacrifice or special exercise of self-denial on the part of the members of society in general to further such endeavours by adopting a political creed of the kind.

No nation that is not prepared to accept and act up to such principles of government can hope to make progress in material prosperity, importance, and civilisation.

I will close this volume by stating that towards the people of the River Plate as a whole, with many of whom I have been brought into frequent contact, and among whom I have several highly valued friends, I am actuated by nothing but kindly feelings.

I also willingly bear testimony to the fact that those countries can boast of numerous members of the bench and bar, of the military service, and of civilians in every walk of life, able and upright men of the highest type, respected by every one who knows them.

Theirs might be one of the bright and prosperous regions of the earth if only the demon of political revolution and discord were exorcised and banished from their lands for ever.

www.ingramcontent.com/pod-product-compliance
Lightning Source LLC
Chambersburg PA
CBHW031328230426
43670CB00006B/275